# Metrospiritual

# Metrospiritual

## *The Geography of Church Planting*

S EAN  B ENESH

RESOURCE *Publications* · Eugene, Oregon

METROSPIRITUAL
The Geography of Church Planting

Resource Publications
An Imprint of Wipf and Stock Publishers
199 W. 8th Ave., Suite 3
Eugene, OR 97401

www.wipfandstock.com

ISBN 13: 978-1-60899-943-9

Manufactured in the U.S.A.

*To Katie, Grant, Camden, Seth, and Mom.*
*Thanks for your love and encouragement!*

# Contents

# Foreword

During the ancient periods of history, some cultures of people decided to stop roaming around as smaller bands, tribes, and clans and started to live together in bigger groups in a permanent place. There are many known examples of cities in the ancient period that are now famous as pivotal shapers of the history of humankind. Structures were erected in key places like crossroads or waterways of transportation and sources of fresh water, and people changed their culture from rural values to more urban thinkers as people of various cultures started to live together in close proximity. This affected every aspect of the social spectrum: politics, business, government, commerce, marriage and family, law, art, education, food, technology, and religion. Urban dwelling especially affected relationships, and the way people conceived community. Consequently, cities still are the pivotal shapers of our culture, both nationally and globally. Dr. Sean Benesh has given us a fresh lens and perspective to look at this reality in his first book, *Metrospiritual*.

From the ancient periods until our 21st century present, some factors have remained a constant, and some have evolved in the way urban dwellers live and relate to each other. The concept of "relationship" is how I would like to start my comments on the ideas Sean wrote in this book. I have known Sean long enough to witness his personal evolution in this passion of his expertise. When I first met Sean, his life was in transition, reflecting the evolution of his values. Sean's developmental years were truly rooted in a rural culture, a culture that he loved even after he went away to college. As a young adult, he was attracted to many things offered by cities, yet still he longed for a flavor of the rural, so he first migrated to a suburb. Suburbs have an interesting history of development all of their own, but most cities are surrounded by communities which try to have the best of both worlds, all of the attractive benefits of a city, while still holding onto some parts of the rural which are foundational to the suburban resident.

Sean lived and ministered in this setting for several years. However, when I met him he was in transition. Sean was experiencing the very phenomenon that at is the heart of Metrospiritual. He was being attracted more and more to the urban culture of the city and less enchanted by sections of the city which still tried to hold onto vestiges of the rural. Yet, strangely enough the cycle of life has caused urban people to struggle with the core of what makes us human, which is being relational in a meaningful way. Sean Benesh is a missiologist looking at this urban evolution and has made fresh observations about how to live out relationships that are intentionally spiritually rich. I have been his friend long enough to watch the evolution of his thoughts that resulted in relocating his life to more and more urban settings. Sean prayerfully moved his family from a small city to a gateway urban center that has a global influence. In doing so, he was simultaneously studying urban issues, formally and informally, and reflecting on the implications of the truths of his personal journey, which is actually a global trend.

Sean has spoken in many of my classes through the years and I have observed his ideas being birthed by excellent teachers and material he has studied, but then refined and matured as he reflected on these truths in the context of ministry and missions. Sean has put a fresh perspective on the application of the urban reality in this era of history. Sean intentionally spent several years studying the urban context from many perspectives: historically, spiritually, missiologically, socially, economically, and many more ways. When Sean researched his dissertation, he took some ideas that many were thinking separately and started to put them together in a fresh new perspective. That work was seminal in the material he has put together in this book, and I was privileged to observe Sean's expertise firsthand while serving on his committee.

Another truth I appreciate is that this work reflects Sean's value for being a learner. In the Kingdom of God some things stay the same and some things have evolved. Truth, love, and other characteristics of God stay the same. However, the concept of the Kingdom that was introduced to us by Jesus and later elaborated on by the Holy Spirit to the early church are things that evolved. The influential churches in the Kingdom were in urban areas, and Peter and Paul had to evolve in their spiritual values to allow for God's idea of mission to be accepted for all the people (panta ta ethne) as this idea evolved through the Books of Acts and the rest of the New Testament. In the spirit of this teachable attitude, Sean has grown and evolved in his personal knowledge and practice to a place that he can now be a teacher to us all in the principles which are presented in this book. Because he has been teachable, he is now our teacher.

In our friendship relationship, Sean has always been transparent. He continues this virtue in this book, and it is part of what metrospirituality means. He is on a journey and is not afraid to ask dozens of questions and only partially answer a few of them. This book is a journey of one person that is a paradigm of what is happening to a whole new generation of urban dwellers who also are followers of Jesus. This is a book about relationships. It is about a person having relationship with God. It is about having a loving relationship with your city as a corporate being. It is about how we love ourselves and define our families in this setting. It is a book about having a biblical relationship with the other people who are our neighbors. In my own book, I use the terms of micro- and macro-community. Metrospirituality is about how to have a relationship with both ideas of communities of people.

The truths of this book are not new; they are as old as the ancients. The way these truths are arranged and communicated by Sean Benesh is new and fresh, and his perspective is pivotal. A metrospiritual concept is that in the 21$^{st}$ century, the ideas that come from the urban context will affect our global culture as much as the urban technology and innovations of the past. The ideas are as real as any architectural monument, and turn the heads of future generations. Sean has given us some tools to use and some questions to reflect upon. Along the way he has mixed in great facts and research to give a foundation for his thoughts. Sean writes as if you are listening to his thoughts, in places like a stream of consciousness journal that has been edited well. Sean calls this a journey. I am glad I'm on it with him.

Dr. Allan Karr
Associate Professor of Missiology and Church Planting
Golden Gate Baptist Theological Seminary
Co-Author, *Church Turned Inside-Out*

# Preface

I could see the whole park from the bench. Sunday mornings usually found me gathering for worship somewhere, but since I had accepted the challenge of moving into this urban neighborhood, I spent lots of time contemplating how I would go about planting a church in the midst of what was a foreign place to me.

I saw the man walking across the park. I had my head down in order to avoid him. My dog, however, was more hospitable. Ed sat down next to me and asked my name. I responded briefly, "Cam."

"Do you want a beer?" he asked. I could see the case of 24 under his arm. Not my usual habit on Sunday morning, so I declined.

"Where do you live?" asked a half hearted me.

"Well, my wife kicked me out because of my drinking. Now I sleep in the dumpster behind the gas station at the mall," said Ed.

"Well I am the new Pastor at the church on the corner. Why don't you come by some morning and I will take you to breakfast." I left, only to get to the edge of the park and God hammered me with, "If you think you are going to plant a church in this neighborhood with an attitude like that—think again!" A lightning bolt would have been less painful.

That was my inauguration into the Edmonds neighborhood. Thankfully, since then, I have adopted a different approach. I am quite sure God has to teach me many times over about his love for the lost in that place and what it meant to have a theology of place. I needed to learn to not only love my neighbors but a neighborhood . . . and then a region, and a city. Over the years I needed to then learn what it meant to train others to do the same and to help in the planting of many other churches in neighborhoods and cities across Canada. Since that time with Ed, almost twenty years ago, I have had the privilege of being a part of four congregations our church has planted, been involved in training many young leaders and pastors through Forge Canada and facilitated a church planting movement across the country under the banner of Church

Planting Canada. I love the church. I love my neighborhood. I love the city. I love Canada.

I tell you all that because of the fact that, although I have learned many things, I have become extremely picky and protective. Only correct motives and a strategy that originates in a deep understanding of theology is good enough for me. As I Pastor, or as the leader of Forge Canada or Church Planting Canada, I am ruthless in my approach to seeing churches planted in every neighborhood. But not just any kind of church—churches that are producing missionaries and not inadvertently producing more of a brand of consumer Christianity. Christians that are not just casual in their approach to life in Christ but understand their calling to participate in the mission of God in their neighborhoods.

In order to do this, we need to change our approach to planting churches. No longer are the old church planting systems sufficient for the culture in which we find ourselves. Doing the demographics and then planning a strategy for how we will attract people to our new service falls woefully short of producing the kind of congregations we need in order to reach our neighborhoods. We need a new way of understanding both the make-up of our neighborhoods, and how we discern what God is doing in these neighborhoods so that we might join him in what he is already doing there.

Sean Benesh gets it. He is not trying to promote a new program that will help us to plant more churches in the postmodern contexts of many cities across North America, but present a series of values and principles that will help us to plant a certain kind of church. It is a church that will reflect a theological depth that reflects the nature of the God we serve. Sean combines both a theology of place, with a theology of the city. We need to counteract White Flight to the suburbs and recognize God's activity in the city and join him in mission there. He has correctly understood the need for us to start in the city, and move towards the suburbs. He points out the need to redefine our measurements of success, instead learning what it means to be faithful in each location. He grapples with many of the most crucial planting issues, and with a number of emerging theological issues that threaten to be at the front of all church discussions over the next generation. He gets what Missional Theology is all about.

There is a growing divide in church circles in my context of Canada. The United States is a little behind Canada in terms of secularization. The church in Canada has been forced to try and learn to adapt to a changing culture. Many have tried to stay put and to recapture the church's place in the midst of the culture that was experienced several generations ago. Others have moved away from the institutional church and towards an emerging model and yet appear to have abandoned the church. What we need more than anything else is for a group of leaders to begin to articulate the importance of recapturing not our place in the culture, but our identity in the fact that we are the people of God. We are not in need of becoming more relevant to the culture, but in becoming more like our Father who has called us to be "in" but not "of" the culture. We are in need of people who will push us towards understanding how God is already at work, and how we are to be the hands and feet of Jesus on our streets, and in our parks, and with our neighbors.

Buckle up, for Sean pushes hard to examine some of our long held presuppositions and to imagine a new way of approaching the planting of churches in the midst of a neglected mission field.

Cam Roxburgh,
*Director of Forge Canada and Church Planting Canada*

# Acknowledgments

Any project of this magnitude is not a solo endeavor. In many ways, this is the culmination of a lifetime of education, ministry opportunities, theological reflection, and exposure to God's heart and plan for the global city. It is also likened to an arrow shot forward as it sets a possible trajectory for further research, education, projects, contemplation, exploration, and writing. There is no denying the reality that what follows in the pages to come is a synthesis of what has been poured into me by many influences as well as influential people. Without these people there is no way I neither would nor could have completed my doctoral dissertation which led to this book.

The first person I would like to acknowledge is Dr. Ron Rushing, who was a professor during my four years at Grace University. Not only did I take nearly every class he taught, but he modeled to me what it means to love God, to be a godly husband and father, and to love and enjoy the academic side of life. Under his influence I grew hungry to learn and, more importantly, to apply what I was soaking in to my life. He was a great mentor, who invested in my life far beyond the classroom.

Next, it was Dr. Linus Morris who taught the first course that I took at Simpson University for my Master's program, which happened to be on church planting. Through that class and his encouragement a new course for my life was set, the path of church planting, a path I have been on since.

I would like to thank David Mann whom I met initially when I was a church planter in Tucson, Arizona. He influenced me in more ways that he could have imagined. His decision to hire me as a church planting strategist changed my life more than almost any other decision thus far. It was through that experience that my eyes were opened for the first time to the city, which caused me to go searching widely about understanding it, what God thinks about it, how I'm to live life as a follower of Jesus in it, and most importantly to fall in love with it. Ultimately this journey led me to Bakke Graduate University in Seattle for doctoral studies. Not only did that decision to become a city-wide church planting strategist change me, but it was through David's encouragement, which he demonstrated by channeling funds to this educational pursuit through his late uncle's endowment. When I filled out the application for BGU I had no idea how I would pay for it. I prayed, "Lord, I want to do this, and if you're behind this you need to provide miraculously." Through this endowment as well as through BGU grants I was able to complete this degree without any out of pocket expense.

I want to thank Dr. Ron Boyce for his guidance and encouragement. The one class I had under him at BGU challenged my assumptions and the way I viewed cities like never before. He taught me to begin seeking to understand the history and nature of the city thus giving me a deeper love and appreciation for it. It was also Dr. Boyce's influence and help that forged the direction of my dissertation and ultimately this book. He worked with me to refine and refine again my methodology of research.

I would also like to thank Dr. Allan Karr. Not only did he help me in the academic arena, but, more importantly, he would let me speak to his church planting students at Golden Gate Baptist Theological Seminary in Mill Valley, California. The best part was trekking across San Francisco in search for some obscure ethnic restaurant to eat at with him and his students. It was through his influence that I learned more about how community transformation and church planting go hand in hand.

Every child is a product of their parents. It was our parents who encouraged us to keep going when we faced defeat, doubt, challenges, and obstacles while growing up. My mom was and forever will be my hero. My mom was a wonderful mother of four busy children all the while she worked full-time and went to school full-time. She was a great model and example to me as an adult as I found myself in the same role of raising children, working full-time and going to school full-time. At a time when I thought I would not be able to go any further on my doctorate, she not only encouraged me but even paid for the rest of my program. I will forever be indebted.

I want to thank Katie and our wonderful boys: Grant, Camden, and Seth. Writing is not something that is quick and easy. It comes with nothing but hard work and long hours. As I came down the home stretch there were a many a nights where I'd be researching and typing away until midnight at the local coffee shop on my dissertation and book. They have sacrificed much to allow me to do this. I know it was challenging at times, but I hope you saw that I did it because of my love for God, my love for you, and how I wanted to be an example that dreams are indeed worth pursuing.

Special thanks to Pebbles Jacobo of A&P Virtual Enterprises who not only helped me tremendously in this project but is a fellow college alum from the same school (Grace University in Omaha). Also, thanks to all of the church planters throughout the West who filled out surveys and helped me collect my data. You took the time and gave me the gift of valuable information and data that proved to be the backbone of this book.

When I showed up on campus my freshman year in college I was a brand new Christian. I did not know much of anything biblically, except that indeed God loves me and has a plan for my life. It was during that time when I decided that I would get a doctorate someday and hopefully begin to write. It is humbling to now look back to see this dream, which was in embryonic form, now become a reality. To God be the glory.

# Introduction

There is no denying it: the world population is flooding to the cities as the pace of urbanization and globalization continues to gain momentum at unprecedented speed. In American cities during the 1950s and 1960s, as their cores became run down and people of different ethnic groups moved in, a phenomenon known as "White Flight" took place where many Caucasians, moved to the sprawling suburbs. Along with that migratory shift arose an emphasis on planting churches in the suburbs to keep pace with the explosive growth. As the success of these new growing suburban churches like Willow Creek and Saddleback began to gain popularity and capture the imagination of church planters and churches alike, so increased the emphasis on church planting in like settings.

However, the dynamics of post-industrial cities began to change again as the economic emphasis shifted from manufacturing to more of a creative economy built around high-tech jobs, the arts, education, and the sciences. Urban cores that were laid waste because of suburban migration resulted in urban decay. Fast forward a few decades and these same neighborhoods are being revitalized on various levels and at differing paces, whether through gentrification or the economic initiatives of the city (or both). As suburbs sprawl further from the city's core, many have opted to move back into the city, whether for a shorter commute time or for aesthetic and cultural preferences. Indeed the momentum now has begun to shift back to urban cores, especially among the growing classification of people dubbed "the Creative Class."

With church planting emphases still leaning towards a suburban bias, the trends for where to start churches are still slow to shift back to the city. This slow shift became especially evident in the years while I served as a church planting strategist for the metro region of Tucson, Arizona. One of my roles was to be a recruiter and catalyst to find and assess potential church planters, whether they lived locally or in some other part of the state or country. Over the span of a few years I noticed a trend among the potential church planters. Most felt called, led, or drawn to plant churches in suburban contexts. In my thinking, church planting began to resemble a donut in cities with activity (frosting) on the outside but nothing on the inside. This new reality began to haunt me as I started the journey to figure out why.

The scope of this book is to investigate the geography of church planting, to find out where churches have been planted since the year 2000 in seven different western cities in North America. Within this context there will be an emphasis on looking at churches starting in gentrified neighborhoods among the Creative Class. Not only that but are new churches engaged in community transformation regardless of where they are planted and if so, then in what ways? I tackle numerous questions that are pertinent to where churches are being planted and why. How did church planters make the decision on site selection for where they planted a church? What influenced them? How are these new churches engaged in community transformation? If they're in gentrified neighborhoods how are they engaging the Creative Class with the Gospel, both in word and deed? Throughout this book these questions and more will be presented, explored, and answered based upon research and the collection of applicable data. Finally, I explore what I call a "metrospirituality," which is an urban-centric faith. In other words, what does it means to live out faith as followers of Jesus in the city and to be engaged in church planting and community transformation in these settings?

As the data was being collected and compiled, questions like, "so what?" arose on numerous occasions. Does it matter or not where new churches are being planted? Is there an identifiable pattern, leaning, or preference? On a more subterranean level these questions raise more questions around the issues of calling because if everyone is equally called by God to plant churches, why are there blatant parts of the city that are neglected and overlooked? Does God care about these people and places as well? The hope is that a book like this will shed light on where churches are being planted and why.

Transformational leaders who adhere to this metrospirituality use power and influence in godly ways to impact their surrounding contexts for the advancement of the Gospel and the betterment of those who live there. In the realm of church planting, stewarding this power and responsibility can lead to community transformation as individuals and even neighborhoods are renewed and redeemed physically, spiritually, and socially. This transformation goes beyond simply easy believism where following Jesus is about adhering to a set of beliefs. Instead, it ought to change everything.

> If you ask most people what Christians believe, they can tell you, "Christians believe that Jesus is God's Son and that Jesus rose from the dead." But if you ask the average person how Christians live, they are struck silent. We have not shown the world another way of doing life. Christians pretty much live like everybody else; they just sprinkle a little Jesus along the way. And doctrine is not very attractive, even if it's true. Few people are interested in a religion that has nothing to say to the world and offers them only life after death, when what people are really wondering is whether there is life before death.[1]

The ramifications of this book may help those who influence church planting over a city or region to be more thoughtful or even proactive when it comes to the site selection on where to start new churches. Along with that influence, these ideas built from research will give church planting leaders more to think about as they're assessing potential church planters and helping them wrestle through issues of calling and the geographic location of where they're to start a new church.

Planting churches is a messy and arduous task, and it varies in degrees of difficulty within the context of the city. Metrospiritual leaders, especially those in gentrifying neighborhoods, have an enormous opportunity and responsibility. They live with one foot in one world and the other foot in another. A neighborhood going through gentrification often times is at a crossroads and a pivotal time in its history. How does a metrospiritual leader as a church planter use leverage to advocate for the lower income and less fortunate in these neighborhoods, all the while encouraging and supporting the renewal process that is cleaning up and bolstering the neighborhood as more people and businesses are moving back into the city? These leaders stand at the intersection of relationships with key city leaders, local citizens, business owners, educators, the non-profit sector, and so much more. They have a rich opportunity to steward this influence and power for the betterment of those involved as well as successive generations.

Here begins the journey to uncover the geography of church planting as well as the motivation behind it and to look at gentrified neighbor-

1. Claiborne, *The Irresistible Revolution*, xix.

hoods and the relationships between church planting, the Creative Class, and community transformation. Like a journey, this one begins with setting the foundation and the background, which gives this book scope and perspective. Dealing with topics such as these can easily fall into the heady realm of pure academia. The goal here is to balance presenting a viable academic work with a more fluid and off-the-cuff writing style that is more at home in the blogosphere. Welcome to the journey of uncovering a metrospirituality and understanding the geography of church planting.

# 1

# Cultural Foundations

Humanity is not some static, unchanging stationary group of people spread out across the globe. Instead, humanity is a dynamic migratory people that move and shift daily. A brief look at human history finds that people are continuously migrating, adapting, and learning. Much of this was done throughout history with varying degrees of contact from one people group to another, and one culture to another. Fast forward to today in the twenty-first century and this global phenomenon of intersecting with other cultures and the shifting migrations of people is at a rapid frantic pace unparalleled in all of human history.

Currently, with the aid of technology such as computers, the internet, television, and cell phones coupled with rapid transportation, the reality of this intersection and migration is evident every single day. For example, I can sit in a coffee shop in Vancouver, British Columbia, who's creation was influenced by Italian espresso cafes, drink tea that originated in China, listen to an internet radio station out of India (yet half of the lyrics are English), wear clothes made in Mexico, type on a computer made by an American company but assembled in Malaysia with tech support based out of India, in a room full of visible minorities (where I'm actually the minority) mostly from East Asia where I'm hearing multiple languages and rarely English, and lastly through instant messaging, email, and chats I am communicating today with people from all over the United States and Canada as well as Central Asia. In the not too distant past this experience would have been utterly mind-boggling for an everyday world citizen, but today it is just as normative as breathing. It has become an involuntary reality in everyday life, especially in urban environments.

Thomas Friedman writes about this process of globalization, which he purports to have a flattening effect on the world in regards to worldwide competition and collaboration. "Because it is flattening and shrinking the world, Globalization 3.0 is going to be more and more driven not only by individuals but also by a much more diverse—non-Western, non-white—group of individuals."[1] Truly, the world is changing at a break-neck pace.

Along with this rapid change is a wholesale people migration like never before, as cities are swelling at an alarming rate. Urbanization means the removal of the rural characteristics of a town or area, a process associated with the development of civilization and technology. Demographically, the term denotes redistribution of populations from rural to urban settlements. As this happens the landscape of cities are changing drastically and human needs grow exponentially. This change has affected the migration patterns in the United States and Canada. "In the U.S., 78 percent of our population is in urban areas."[2]

Not only are cities growing, but they're diversifying as a myriad of ethnic groups and nationalities from around the world collect in pockets across urban centers. For example, in Vancouver, British Columbia, 47.1 percent of the population is "visible minorities" with most coming from Asia.[3] Also, Los Angeles is known as being an incredibly diverse city. "The diverse, multiethnic population of Los Angeles today distinguishes the city as the cultural hub of the Pacific Rim... People from about 140 countries, speaking approximately 86 different languages, currently call Los Angeles home."[4]

Along with this urbanization, many cities throughout the world are going through the process of gentrification, which is "the process of renewal and rebuilding accompanying the influx of middle-class or affluent people into deteriorating areas that often displaces poorer residents."[5] "Gentrification has gone global and is intertwined with processes of globalization."[6] At the core of many cities all over North America, there is this urban renewal or renaissance taking place, which has and continues to change the fabric of living. Again, it is all part of migratory patterns happening all around.

1. Friedman, *The World Is Flat,* 11.
2. Roberts Jr., *Glocalization,* 61.
3. Wikimedia Foundation Inc., "Demographics of Vancouver."
4. LA Inc., "L.A. Facts."
5. Merriam-Webster, Inc., "Gentrification."
6. Lees et al., *Gentrification,* xvii.

Humanity is changing and adapting, and cities are expanding and diversifying. Things seem to constantly be in flux, and at the same time the church in the West is presented with challenges of adapting and becoming more fluid, just like culture. If the church does not adapt its forms and structures, it will be less and less of a factor as the twenty-first century progresses. In many ways the church has been immersed in an institutional paradigm for 1,700 years in regards to its ecclesiology, which was forever influenced in the fourth century when Christianity became the official religion of the Roman Empire. Although cultures shift and morph the way Christians have done church has changed little, and many changes today are simply cosmetic as the church tweaks music styles, architectural designs, and utilizes technology in worship services. It is viewed as almost scandalous to even think and talk this way.

> Rarely do we hear a serious critique of the often hidden assump-
> tions on which Christendom itself stands. It seems that the tem-
> plate of this highly institutional version of Christianity is so deeply
> embedded in our collective psyche that we have inadvertently put
> it beyond the pale of prophetic critique. We have so divinized this
> mode of church through centuries of theologizing about it that we
> have actually confused it with the kingdom of God, an error that
> seems to have plagued Catholic thinking in particular throughout
> the ages.[7]

In a world that is rapidly changing it is vital for the church to re-gain its missional thrust and look anew at its basic ecclesiology in light of church planting in the central city, which includes gentrified neighborhoods. The goal is not to preserve forms and structures that have been in place throughout church history but allow the basic assumptions, forms, and structures to be fluid, which is vital in a globalizing and urbanizing world. Cities are constantly changing, especially as they go through the various cycles of blight and renewal. Church planting in urban areas and even those that are in this gentrification process reveals that issues of church contextualization and adaptability are key. Every time a new church is planted it is always rooted in context, and most often this dictates the forms and expressions, which is why churches in the city should look different from their suburban counterparts.

7. Hirsch, *The Forgotten Ways*, 51.

The root of my journey into the city began when seemingly out of nowhere one day a few years ago, a previously unrealized reality dawned on me. This light that turned on was the realization that for the most part there was hardly any church planting in the city where I lived and served in compared with the ever-growing suburban fringe. I did not have any preconceived ideas or notions on the geography of church planting when I took on the role as a church planting strategist, but all of a sudden when I transitioned from being a church planter into this role everything changed. My family and I had moved to Tucson, Arizona, to begin the process of planting a church. At that point in my life I was still afraid of cities and did not really care much for them. On the other hand, I did enjoy the suburban fringe as long as I was as far and away from the city center as I could be and close to the mountains and open country. Having grown up in rural Iowa it was this earlier worldview that was still shaping and influencing me. I always tell people how I am urban specialist since I grew up in Iowa because I definitely know what urban is not. While growing up for us to drive to the "big city" was to Marshalltown . . . population 20,000. They actually had a McDonald's and a Burger King!

When we moved to Tucson our team spent the first couple of years planning and launching the church and year after we started our public worship gatherings I was asked to come on staff with our denomination as a regional church planting strategist for the Tucson metro area. That one decision began to change everything. Instead of caring only for my little section of the city in a far-flung suburb, I was all of a sudden given charge to be the catalyst to see churches planted all over the metro area and among the various ethnic groups. At that point I did not really understand cities, nor did I even have a biblical or theological framework for the city in which to look through. Once I became a strategist I knew everything had to change, but wasn't too sure how to begin.

The first thing I did was to muster up all the courage I had to make the 12 mile trek from my house to downtown Tucson. If I was going to begin understanding the city and where to plant churches I figured the most logical place to start was in the downtown core. I had been in Tucson for over two years now, yet ventured downtown once or twice only to quickly pass through it, all the while being extremely uncomfortable and out of my element. Tucson was on the verge on cresting a million in population, but the way the city is laid out it is very horizontal. In this desert setting, since land was cheap, it was rather easy to scrape the desert to make way for housing. As a result the city grew in every seam where there were no mountains. With that being said, Tucson's downtown central city skyline is very small, especially by the standards of cities with a population of a million or more. It did not matter to me though, and with laptop in tow I drove into the city to explore and learn. Through concerted effort I found a parking spot, walked over to a coffee shop, and I was set.

This lone and seemingly simple decision set in motion a trajectory that would change the entire way I looked at and understood cities. It wasn't too long after that when I began to notice where church planting efforts were taking place across the metro area. About a year into my new role I spent time with a number of church planters, as well as prospective church planters who came to Tucson to explore the possibility of planting a church with us. I slowly began to see a trend, which I paid more attention to throughout the following year, leading to new convictions as my ministry began to unfold.

I vividly remember the day it hit me because I wrote a blog called *Jesus Loves White Affluent Suburbanites* on my blog at theurbanloft.org. At that point I probably worked with fifty potential and actual church planters. Without actual documentation, I would venture to say that roughly 80 to 90 percent of them "felt called" to plant churches in the suburbs. I cynically thought to myself, "If God is calling all of these church planters to the suburbs then he must not like ethnic urbanites because he's not calling anyone there." Afterwards, I began doing informal surveys in other cities and the results looked the same over and over again. Thus, my quest began.

Years later after being a regional strategist we moved to Burnaby (Vancouver), British Columbia to jump back into church planting. After planting once and being a strategist, I vowed I would never plant a church again. I had worked with a number of church planters long enough to see grand successes and horrible failures. It is brutal work and causes a lot of soul-searching, especially when one is faced with the impossible task of creating something *ex nihilo*. This time around for me it was different. All of the issues and topics this book focuses on have now come together in one great confluence of church planting in a central city with pertinent issues like gentrification, defining and planting a church among the Creative Class, in a culturally and racially diverse neighborhood where I'm a minority, and exploring the way new churches engage in community transformation. The name of our new church is Ion Community (www.ioncommunity.org) and it is our vision to plant churches across the metro area in each of the city or municipals centers. These are like mini-downtown urban areas spread across the metro area. This plan all goes hand in hand with Vancouver's metro Livable Region Strategic Plan.

In 1996 metro Vancouver adopted the Livable Region Strategic Plan. This plan serves as a framework for effective decision-making for land-use as well as transportation. In summary, it is the creation of a network of regional and municipal city or town centers. What this looks like are numerous distinct "mini-downtowns" spread throughout the metro area. These "mini-downtowns" are then hubs for business, living, and lifestyle amenities. In most cities there is usually the downtown core and every-thing radiates out from that to the edges. The city centers act like a great big lung breathing in people only to breath them back out. Throughout a typical day this "lung" is breathing in and out tens of thousands of people.

What makes Vancouver unique is its view towards urban develop-ment. Immediately apparent is the lack of freeways, which crisscross every other city with more frequency the larger a city gets. Without freeways traffic can be quite congested and slow. The focus of any city is the down-town core. If one were to look at postcards of any city, it usually shows the downtown skyline. When most people think of cities, this picture is their default image. What metro Vancouver started and is in the process of fulfilling is to compact the population into high-density clusters known as "city centers" or "municipal centers." Dotted throughout the metro area are these unique city centers that act as regional hubs for that part of the city.

For example, I live in Burnaby in the Edmonds Town Centre. It looks like its own small downtown with high-rise residential towers and commercial businesses clustered together. Just a mile and a half away is Metrotown, an older and more mature city center with a myriad of similar towers, mega shopping amenities, and plenty of high-rise office towers. While Burnaby is a suburb with close to 250,000 in population, Metrotown has a skyline that is two to three times larger than Tucson's for example. However, Metrotown is only one of four separate city centers in Burnaby, including Edmonds, Lougheed, and Brentwood. It indeed is urban living outside of the downtown core.

Vancouver is an example of Postmodern Urbanism. "Such a city is composed of multiple, differentially interconnected site, arranged in a decentered, nonhierarchical fashion."[8] While we are still in our embryonic stages it is the dream for the Ion Community to plant churches or expressions of Ion in each of the city centers throughout the region beginning in Burnaby. In the same way that these centers are unique yet connected to a larger whole, so will be each expression of the Ion Community. But more importantly the question is not "What is the dream for Ion?" Instead, it is "What is God's dream for our community?" The Ion is simply a vessel or vehicle to bring about community transformation in each of these various hubs.

Like I mentioned before, one of the reasons my family and I chose to begin our first Ion Community in metro Vancouver is because it exemplified the blending together of topics related to this book. This area we currently live in is going through quite a gentrification process as it has become a hub for southeast Burnaby. One morning I was talking with a barista at the new Waves Coffee here that opened not too long ago. She was telling me of her desire to move here, to Edmonds, because now it's a safer place as she wants a closer commute for work. Even two years ago it wasn't that safe of a neighborhood as it had a strong presence of drugs and crime. However, many high-rise towers have recently been built, which has brought a completely different demographic and vibe to the neighborhood. Burnaby, although technically is a suburb, has shifted definitively to an urban environment. Scattered all around the base of these great towers and just across the street are apartments for the lower income. On one side of the street are aesthetically beautiful towers jutting into the sky, yet on the other are run down three story apartments that have seen better days. There's a great mix of socio-economic layers all living and sharing public spaces together.

The other facet of Edmonds Town Centre that stands out, like many parts of metro Vancouver, is the rich diversity. The elementary school our boys attend is a neighborhood school with most of the students coming from the densest part of Edmonds. Roughly 60 to 70 percent of the school children are what Vancouver calls "visible minorities." Most of them are from some country in Asia, whether eastern or southern. Most Caucasians are directly from Europe, particularly from Russia and Eastern Europe.

The diversity found here became apparent rather quickly. One day while waiting to pick our boys up from school, I stood in a cluster of

8. Dear, *From Chicago to L.A.*, 85.

roughly 20 parents. I attentively listened to them talk to one another and found that only about one out of ten were even speaking English. I watched their children walk up the sidewalks with their friends talking in English, but as soon as they got to their parents they began speaking in their mother tongue. There are around one hundred different languages spoken in this area alone.

Another example of Vancouver's diversity I want to share is from the following evening when I was at the neighborhood Waves Coffee while doing some writing. It was eleven o'clock at night and the place was crammed full of mostly young adults. There were between thirty and forty people sitting, drinking coffee, doing homework and talking with friends. I quickly realized that I was the only Caucasian in the entire coffee shop. However, if you were to go to that same place in the morning you would see that about half of the customers were Caucasians. This scenario is typical is my current ministry context.

The trajectory of this book begins with looking at church planting in seven different cities in the Western part of the United States and Canada. It is essential that church planting and urban renewal theory to be planted in context. Too often we speak and write without roots. There were several factors vital to the choosing of these cities. Studying church planting among denominations and networks in large cities can be a daunting task in and of itself. Therefore, I wanted to look at cities that were roughly the same size and that represented the different regions in the West in which I live. Why the West? I wanted to study cities I was familiar with, which would aid in the collection of data. Having familiarity with the cities was important as it afforded me the opportunity to tap into various denominations and church planting networks, as well as church planting leaders that I knew in each city.

As a result, the focus cities are Denver, Albuquerque, Tucson, Phoenix, Portland, Seattle, and Vancouver (BC). Again, these provide context. Whether one lives in Miami or Mumbai, Chicago or Tokyo, Nashville or London, Boston or Beijing, Dallas or Paris, New York or Nairobi, Minneapolis or Lima, or Boise or Berlin, there are common characteristics that apply. With that said, every city is unique and like a fingerprint, no two are alike. I have lived in cities of all different shapes and sizes and found each to be unique. Church planters and agents of urban renewal know their cities best. Some cities are filled with 50 to 70 percent squatters while others house powerful global economies. The population spectrum for the cities I studied ranged roughly between one million to over four million. Cities that would be somewhere on the spectrum of being deemed a world-class city were key to be included, although none of them represented a top tier global city. I avoided certain cities because of the sheer size and complexity of the metro area, like Los Angeles and San Francisco, and some of the cities in which I had far less contacts, including Salt Lake City, Las Vegas, San Diego, and Sacramento. If time were less of a factor it would have been fascinating to expand this study to Latin America, Africa, Europe, and Asia. Listed below are the cities and their respective city proper and metropolitan populations.

1. Vancouver BC–city 578,041; metro 2,116,581[9]
2. Seattle–city 602,000 city; metro 3,344, 813[10]
3. Portland–city 557,706; metro 2,159,720[11]
4. Phoenix–city 1,567,924; metro 4,281,900[12]
5. Tucson–city 541,811; metro 1,023,320[13]
6. Albuquerque–city 521,999, metro 845,913[14]
7. Denver–city 598,707; metro 2,506,626[15]

What it interesting to note is that apart from Phoenix each of the other six cities has roughly the same size of population in the city proper. Also worth mentioning is that the ethnic make-up of the various cities offers interesting insights ranging from the Hispanic influenced cities of the southwest to the Asian influenced cities of the Northwest. To me, this is key since many of the fastest growing urban centers are found in Latin America and Asia. All of the cities studied do hold vital relationships with cities on these continents. With that in mind, I will give a brief overview of each of the cities to provide some background and context for the research.

9. Wikimedia Foundation, Inc., "Vancouver."
10. Wikimedia Foundation, Inc., "Seattle."
11. Wikimedia Foundation, Inc., "Portland, Oregon."
12. Wikimedia Foundation, Inc., "Phoenix, Arizona."
13. Wikimedia Foundation, Inc., "Tucson, Arizona."
14. Wikimedia Foundation, Inc., "Albuquerque, New Mexico."
15. Wikimedia Foundation, Inc., "Denver."

Vancouver, British Columbia is the only focus city that is in Canada. As part of the larger mega-region of Cascadia, along with Seattle and Portland, it was an important addition to the mix as it fit the size parameters, I had ample connections within the metro area and, on a personal level, it is also because we live here. What makes Vancouver interesting as a focus city is that not only is it in Canada, but it is one of the most multicultural cities in the world. Canadian cities are truly unique and different than their American counterparts. Roughly half of the entire metro area is considered a "visible minority" with most being Asian. Immigration has impacted the city almost more than any other factor to date. A church planting missionary, shortly after our arrival to the Vancouver metro area, asked me in jest, "What separates China from India?" I fumbled through my limited geography of Asia to come up with the answer. I was thinking along the lines of Tibet, the Himalayas, or some other obscure country I never heard of. The guy laughed at me when I was trying to answer. The answer? It's the Fraser River here in metro Vancouver. The Fraser River is what separates Vancouver, Richmond, and Burnaby from Surrey. Most Asian immigrants north of the river are Chinese. On the other hand, most of the immigrants in Surrey, south of the river, are Indo-Canadian (from India). Most of those are Sikhs from Punjab and one of the defining cultures here.

Another key factor that makes Vancouver stand out as well is its unique urban expression.

> Vancouver has emerged as the poster child of urbanism in North America. In recent years, through a series of locally grown strategies, Vancouver has consciously willed itself into becoming a model of contemporary city-making. Like the most vivid of dreams, the city is reinventing itself: something curious, perhaps even miraculous, is happening here.[16]

This expression of urban development and design stands in stark contrast to the other six cities in the study. This fact also made it more difficult to distinguish urban from suburban. One of the elements I looked at, in which I go into more detail later, is where churches are being planted. I wanted to see how many were urban (city proper) versus suburban. What makes metro Vancouver a challenge is that because of its

16. Berelowitz, *Dream City*, 1.

unique urbanism influenced by the Livable Region Strategic Plan[17] along with immigration, it is difficult to distinguish urban versus suburban. Most people think of suburban as single family track homes sprawling as far as the eye can see punctuated by strip malls. These characteristics are roughly the same whether talking about suburban Denver, Tucson, or Portland. Vancouver, on the other hand, is much different although there are those characteristics the further out one drives.

Burnaby, where I live, is considered a suburb of Vancouver as it borders the city on its eastern flank. However, Burnaby is hardly suburban according to the way most think about it. Even on the City of Burnaby's website they consider themselves urban.[18] The website tracks the city's history and development from rural to suburban to urban. There are more high-density high-rise residential and commercial towers in Burnaby (population 250,000) than most cities in the United States that are multiple times its size. One can live in Burnaby and still live a very urban lifestyle. In determining what percentage of churches planted were in urban or suburban settings was a bit more of a challenge to differentiate in metro Vancouver so I simply stuck with classic demarcations.

Moving south across the Canadian and U.S. border the next focus city is Seattle, Washington. Roughly 70 percent of the population is Caucasian with the next largest demographic segment being Asian at 13.5 percent, African Americans make up about 8 percent of the population, and Hispanics comprise of 6 percent.[19] Included in the metro population are the cities of Tacoma (197,000) and Bellevue (123,000), which blur the lines between urban and what is suburban. For example, Bellevue, with its rapidly changing downtown, has the second largest city center in Washington.[20] Downtown Tacoma is also going through its own renaissance and included in the core is the state's first electric light rail system.[21] Both of these city centers are very much urban in feel, characteristics, and culture.

Seattle is a great focus city to look at with its high rankings on the Creativity Index and presence of the Creative Class, as well as the activity

17. Metro Vanvcouver, "Livable Centres."
18. The City of Burnaby, "Welcome to Burnaby."
19. Wikimedia Foundation, Inc., "Seattle Demographics."
20. Wikimedia Foundation, Inc., "Bellevue, Washington."
21. Wikimedia Foundation, Inc., "Tacoma, Washington."

of several very strong church planting organizations. Seattle is a magnet for the Creative Class, whether it's the draw of such companies as Microsoft or Amazon, cool gentrified neighborhoods like Capitol Hill, Belltown, or South Lake Union, the fact that it is the coffee capital, there is an abundance of outdoor and cultural amenities, or because of the music scene, Seattle is a cool city. One such hotspot is South Lake Union,[22] which sits on the north end of downtown. Currently going through a massive revitalization and gentrification process, it is one of the largest urban renewal projects in the United States. Although it is known for being one of the most under-churched cities in the United States, Seattle has a strong recent history of a flurry of new church plants driven by the Acts 29 Network and the Puget Sound Baptist Association (Seattle Church Planting).

Further down the Pacific Northwest and rounding out the Cascadia mega-region is Portland, Oregon. Portland is the third most populous city in the Pacific Northwest behind Seattle and Vancouver BC. Out of all Portland's population roughly 70 percent of were Caucasian followed by 8.5 percent Hispanic, 6.7 percent Asian, and 6.6 percent African American.[23] Some have labeled Portland as the Whitest city in the United States of a city its size. Held up as a model of the new urbanism, Portland is also the least racially diverse city in the group of focus cities. An article called "The White City," on the New Geography website, explains:

> Among the media, academia and within planning circles, there's a generally standing answer to the question of what cities are the best, the most progressive and best role models for small and mid-sized cities. The standard list includes Portland, Seattle, Austin, Minneapolis, and Denver. In particular, Portland is held up as a paradigm, with its urban growth boundary, extensive transit system, excellent cycling culture, and a pro-density policy. These cities are frequently contrasted with those of the Rust Belt and South, which are found wanting, often even by locals, as "cool" urban places. But look closely at these exemplars and a curious fact emerges. If you take away the dominant Tier One cities like New York, Chicago and Los Angeles you will find that the "progressive" cities aren't red or blue, but another color entirely: white.[24]

22. Wikimedia Foundation, Inc., "South Lake Union."
23. Wikimedia Foundation, Inc., "Portland, Oregon Demographics."
24. Renn, "The White City."

The decision to add Portland as one of the focus cities was mainly because of their label as being a progressive city, which is a hotbed not only for issues like new urbanism, creative city planning, and gentrification, but also because it is a haven for the Creative Class. Portland is a great model city for many because of its revitalized downtown core, investment in a light rail system, their land-use planning strategy, and the city's progress towards being an eco-friendly and sustainable city. With its abundance of gentrified neighborhoods full of coffee shops and micro-breweries, Portland is a perfect city to study church planting in.

Phoenix, Arizona is an interesting case study among cities, especially among the focus cities. It seems like in many ways it is the story of a city that exploded onto the scene with rapid growth and far-reaching sprawl, only to find it going back to the basics of revamping the transportation infrastructure and carving out its own unique urban expression. The city was born in the hot, dry, flat Salt River Valley in between numerous small mountain ranges on the northeastern tip of the Sonoran Desert. The city is, in my view, a very horizontal city because instead of building up (compact and dense) the city, they kept moving further away from the city center due to cheap land. However, because of influences such as new urbanism and skyrocketing fuel prices, the city has begun reinvesting in its downtown core. Not only that, but Phoenix is creating a great infrastructure that includes a light rail system[25] to carry people to city center from the suburbs. Like any sprawling city traffic congestions on the freeways is an issue.

Non-Hispanic Caucasians comprise of 48 percent of the population, while Hispanics make up 41.5 percent (or one could say Phoenix is 75 percent Caucasian American, which does include "Hispanic Caucasians"). By far Phoenix's city proper is the largest of any of the focus cities, sitting just over 1,500,000, which makes it the fifth largest city in the United States. With its metro population at 4,200,000, it is the twelfth largest metro in the United States.

Having lived in the Phoenix area for three years, it is a city I am quite familiar with, which is why it was added into the list of focus cities. Not only that, but with the city's reinvestment in the downtown, Phoenix is seeing numerous neighborhoods gentrified, attracting more of the Creative Class. The idea that Phoenix is simply a retirement city or a place

---

25. Valley Metro, "Metro Light Rail."

for winter visitors is slowly giving way to Phoenix as a progressive city scratching and clawing its way onto the global scene.

Just an hour and a half south of Phoenix and sitting sixty miles north of the Mexican border is Tucson. For the most part, Tucson is a classic grid city, which makes for great ease in getting around. Having been built in a flat basin hemmed in by several mountain ranges, the grid system works well. When the city flows into the foothills of the surrounding mountain ranges, the grid system is set aside and it simply follows the contours of the slopes. This situation is where more creativity and beauty abounds as far as a cityscape.

Tucson's non-Hispanic Caucasian population is 50 percent and Hispanics make up roughly 40 percent of the population. The metro's population just recently crested the million mark in 2007, which is giving the city renewed optimism about the future. The city has a bright future, indeed, in front of it along with some key obstacles to overcome. According to one city planner, the way the city reaches two million people in population must be different from the way it got to one million. The city planners have taken trips to other cities such as Portland to learn about the land-use planning and how to stem the tide of sprawl.

When the San Presidio Augustin de Tucson was first established in 1775 the original part of the city more resembled an ancient Spanish city with open courtyards and streets. It was a walled city for the protection of the soldiers and their families from the raiding Apaches. Tucson would not make the ancient city planners of Hippodamus or Hippocrates very happy if they were to walk the streets of it today. It's a sprawling city recuperating from the effects of uncontrolled growth. The street level scene is one of the worst features in Tucson. One of the major cross-town roads, Speedway Boulevard, was voted in the 1970s as the ugliest street in America.

There are a numerous bright spots in the built environment that would make some of these early Greek planners and philosophers content. Main Gate Square[26] is a great example of the new urbanism with its wide sidewalks, aesthetically beautiful streetscape, and walkable neighborhoods. The downtown is on the front end of revitalization as they seek to apply this new urbanism to beautify and draw people back to the city core. On top of that many of the newer sub-developments on the fringe

26. The Marshall Foundation, "Main Gate Square."

of the city are indeed aesthetically appealing with an abundance of open space, parks, greenbelts, and homes that seek to blend into the desert surroundings.

The last of the focus cities in the American Southwest and acting as a bridge to the Rocky Mountain states' cities is Albuquerque, New Mexico. With the Rio Grande weaving its way through the city, Albuquerque is a city of contrasts. It sits in the upper reaches of the Chihuahuan Desert, which is a much different desert climate than the other focus cities of Tucson and Phoenix. To the east the Sandia Mountains rise abruptly from the desert floor casting a ubiquitous presence over the city below. In many ways Albuquerque shares a common history as well as topography with Tucson. They're both roughly the same size, both with large universities close to the downtown and air force bases on the south side, hemmed in by jagged mountains on the east, a rich history of Hispanic and Native American influence, and with downtowns in the process of being revital-ized. As a matter of fact, there's some sense of healthy competition between the two cities since they are so similar. Forty percent of Albuquerque is Hispanic and apart from Caucasians roughly four percent of the metro area is Native American.

Most people assume that most of the cities in the West are relatively new compared to the cities in the Midwest and back East, but the reality is that Albuquerque was founded in 1706. Fast forward to the twenty-first century, and the city is making bold strides to rebrand and reinvent itself. "On March 23, 2007, the city's mayor Martin Chavez announced his plan to brand the city 'the Q.'"[27] Some call the mayor's vision a "hip reincarna-tion" of Albuquerque. Like most cities, Albuquerque's downtown core fell on hard times due to neglect and a suburban focus but now that is chang-ing. Along with rebranding, the city is reinvesting in its downtown core, and there are numerous residential developments and redevelopments including lofts and creating trendy districts like EDo (East Downtown). "EDo is a trendy area containing several loft apartment buildings and a number of small shops and restaurants."[28] Not only is there downtown development going on, but other such influences like new urbanism is finding a home in Albuquerque in new developments. "Mesa del Sol is the largest new master-planned, mixed-use, New Urbanist community

27. Ibid.
28. Wikimedia Foundation, Inc., "Downtown Albuquerque."

currently under development in the United States."[29] Located ten miles south of the downtown core the plans call for 100,000 residents and to create and attract 40,000 jobs.

Rounding out the last of the focus cities is Denver, Colorado, as it sits at the base of the Front Range of the Rocky Mountains at its eastern flank. While Albuquerque is at the southern end of the Rockies it is considered more part of the southwest both in geography and culture. Denver, on the other hand, is somewhat of an "island" of sorts, being geographically separated from the other cities. Sitting at somewhat of a crossroads, Denver is the halfway point between Midwest cities like Chicago and St. Louis with the West Coast. The semi-isolation means that Denver is the largest city for 600 miles. With a metro population of 2,500,000 it is the twenty-first largest metro area in the United States. Studying downtowns is vital for this project. It is interesting to note that four out of seven of my focus cities experienced the highest population booms in their downtown cores in the 1990s among all the cities in the United States. "In the 1990s, Brookings found only five downtowns with increases of more than 35 percent: Seattle (77 percent), Denver (51 percent), Colorado Springs (48 percent), Albuquerque (45 percent) and Portland (35 percent)."[30] The article then goes on to say something interesting about who actually lives downtown, particularly in Denver. "But Denver's downtown population tends to be less ethnically or racially diverse than most other downtowns, as was the case with Colorado Springs. Colorado Springs' downtown population was 75.9 percent Caucasian, while Denver's was 74.4 percent."[31]

As far as the ethnic breakdowns of the focus cities, the primary ethnicities next to Caucasians are either Asian or Hispanic. Denver has a Hispanic and Latino population of 32 percent with the next largest segment being African Americans at 10 percent. Denver, of all the focus cities, has the largest percentage of African Americans in the city.

Like most cities gentrification has played a key role in influencing the city and reinvestment in it. Places like gentrified neighborhoods are vital because they're havens for the Creative Class. One such neighborhood in Denver is Capitol Hill,[32] which is the city's most densely populated neigh-

29. Wikimedia Foundation, Inc., "Mesa Del Sol."

30. American City Business Journals, Inc., "Population Boom Seen For Downtown Denver."

31. Ibid.

32. Wikimedia Foundation, Inc., "Capital Hill."

borhood. As typical for older neighborhoods, it was once the haven for the social elite dating back to the nineteenth century. Over time the area was increasingly neglected with drugs and prostitution becoming more commonplace. In recent history artists and musicians began moving in calling the area home. Gentrification has caught up with Capitol Hill with its popularity and proximity to the central business district. However, with the double-edged sword of gentrification, there are challenges on many fronts. Many lower income families are being priced right out of the rental homes, and there's a culture clash between the resident bohemians, artists, and musicians with the incoming influx of higher income people. Also, along with many gentrified neighborhoods that attract the Creative Class, Capitol Hill is a gay-friendly neighborhood.

With its unique topography and geography, proximity to the mountains with ample outdoor activities, vibrant downtown core with many cultural amenities, strong economy, and gentrifying neighborhoods, Denver makes a great addition to the list of focus cities with its large Creative Class.

## THE CREATIVE CLASS

One of the elements of this book is to take a look at the Creative Class in each of the selected focus cities. It is no surprise that hip and progressive cities, particularly those out West that I'm looking at, are also havens for the Creative Class because of the various factors that draw them there. There also seems to be a direct correlation between cities with revitalized and hip central cities and the presence of this economic and lifestyle group of people. Since my studies and research focuses partly on church planting not only within the city limits and the downtown core, but also in gentrified neighborhoods, an explanation of the Creative Class is necessary since this is who often time lives there and fuels gentrification.

Who is the Creative Class? "The Creative Class is a socioeconomic class that economist and social scientist Richard Florida, a professor and head of the Martin Prosperity Institute at the Rotman School of Management at the University of Toronto, identifies as a key driving force for economic development of post-industrial cities in the USA."[33] According to Florida, the Creative Class is comprised of around forty-million workers, which make up roughly 30 percent of the entire U.S.

33. Wikimedia Foundation, Inc., "Creative Class."

workforce. "The Creative Class consists of people who add economic value through their creativity."[34] The Creative Class is broken down into two main groupings.

> The distinguishing characteristic of the Creative Class is that its members engage in work whose function is to "create meaning-ful new forms" define the Creative Class as consisting of two components. The Super-Creative Core of this new class includes scientists and engineers, university professors, poets and novelists, artists, entertainers, actors, designers and architects, as well as the thought leadership of modern society: nonfiction writers, editors, cultural figures, think-tank researchers, analysts and other opinion-makers. Whether they are software programmers or engineers, architects or filmmakers, they fully engage in the creative process.[35]

Outside of this Creative Core there is another grouping as well that makes up the Creative Class. These are people who add value to society through using their intellect and creativity.

> Beyond this core group, the Creative Class also includes "creative professionals" who work in a wide range of knowledge-intensive industries such as high-tech sectors, financial services, the legal and health care professions, and business management. These people engage in creative problem solving, drawing on complex bodies of knowledge to solve specific problems. Doing so typically requires a high degree of formal education and thus a high level of human capital.[36]

The Creative Class is drawn to cities that rank high on the 3 T's: talent, technology, and tolerance. "In *Cities and the Creative Class*, Florida devoted several chapters to a discussion of the three main prerequisites of creative cities—though there are many additional qualities that distinguish creative magnets. Basically, for a city to become a magnet for the Creative Class, it must be an example of 'the three 'T's' of Talent (have a highly talented/educated/skilled population), Tolerance (have a diverse community, which has a 'live and let live' ethos), and Technology (have the technological infrastructure necessary to fuel an entrepreneurial culture)."[37]

34. Florida, *The Rise of the Creative Class*, 68.
35. Ibid., 69.
36. Ibid., 69.
37. Ibid., 69.

"Creativity and the members of the Creative Class take root in places that possess all three of these critical factors. Each is a necessary, but by itself insufficient, condition. To attract creative people, generate innovation, and stimulate economic development, a place must have all three."[38]

One of the reasons behind the interest in the Creative Class for many city leaders and companies is that often times they are great drivers of the local economy. It is believed that the larger the number of creative types in a city the greater the economic outlook is. This factor is why cities that rank high on the Creativity Index are also known for such things as a robust economy, hipness, and progressiveness. The Creativity Index was created by Richard Florida as a way to evaluate a city's overall creativity, innovation, and openness.

> The Creativity Index is a mix of four equally weighted factors: (1) the Creative Class share the workforce; (2) innovation, measured as patents per capita; (3) high-tech industry, using the Milken Institute's widely accepted Tech Pole Index (which I refer to as the High-Tech Index); and (4) diversity, measured by the Gay Index, a reasonable proxy for an area's openness to different kinds of people and ideas. This composite indicator is a better measure of a region's underlying creative capabilities than the simple measure of the Creative Class, because it reflects the joint effects of its concentration and of innovative economic outcomes.[39]

Of the six U.S. cities looked at in this research, the lowest ranking on the Creativity Index was a thirty-two. Two of the cities ranked in the top ten, with Seattle at number three and Portland at number seven. The rankings are as following:[40]

1. #3–Seattle

2. #7–Portland

3. #11–Albuquerque

4. #14–Denver

5. #28–Phoenix

6. #32–Tucson

7. N/A–Vancouver BC

38. Florida, *Cities and the Creative Class*, 37.
39. Florida, *The Rise of the Creative Class*, 244–45.
40. Ibid., 356–57.

The range of rankings is out of roughly 270 cities, which means that each of my focus cities as a whole, is in the upper echelon of creative cities. Seattle and Portland are in the top two percent of all American cities that range in population anywhere from small metros of under 250,000 to large ones over 1,000,000. Even Tucson with its "low" ranking compared to the other focus cities is still higher than roughly 240 other cities across the United States. What is interesting to note is the correlation between the Creativity Index and cities with rapidly revitalizing and gentrifying central cities and urban neighborhoods. This phenomenon is drawing people back to live in the city, as noted in the Brookings report earlier in this chapter with Denver, Albuquerque, Seattle, and Portland having the fastest percentage of population growth in their central cities.

Cities that have been exposed to and bought into Florida's research are scrambling over one another in an attempt to draw or retain this class in their cities. In some ways it is the new arms race for U.S. and Canadian cities and global cities alike. Whoever rebrands and reinvents themselves first and bolsters their creative economy to make it favorable to draw and retain this class wins. What does the winner get? A stronger economy and brighter future; therefore, it is no small task in front of them. Florida asserts there is almost a tipping point for the relationship between the Creative Class and a robust economy with an abundance of knowledge or creative-based companies. "Creative people and companies cluster because of the powerful productivity advantages, economies of scale, and knowledge spillovers such density brings."[41] That clustering effect is why all of the cities on my list of focus cities are going to great ends to draw this class or keep them if they're already present. "The rise of the creative economy radically alters the ways that cities and regions establish and maintain competitive advantage."[42] Every city studied is somewhere on the continuum of revitalizing their downtown core whether they're at the beginning, mid-way, or have been plodding along quite some time. One of the motivations is to appeal to this class who value the city and many of its cultural and lifestyle amenities over a more suburban lifestyle.

As an example, Tucson's downtown, which will soon be featuring a new modern street car system, is also retrofitting older buildings making them into attractive lofts for creative types and young professionals.

41. Florida, *Who's Your City*, 30.
42. Florida, *Cities and the Creative Class*, 39.

Tucson never had a large downtown, but due to influences such as new urbanism and the presence of the Creative Class they're seeking to tap into these movements to help revitalize the downtown. The downtown is positioned well to do so given the close proximity to the University of Arizona and other creative havens, such as Fourth Avenue, which is located between the downtown and the university. University settings are magnets and producers of creative types. Often times they create a clustering dynamic. "In my view, the presence of a major research university is a basic infrastructure component of the Creative Economy—more important than the canals, railroads and freeway systems of past epochs—and a huge potential source of competitive advantage."[43] What Tucson aims to do is to link the downtown with Fourth Avenue, the University of Arizona, and the University Medical Center together. Who benefits? Suburban families? No, people who live downtown around the university district who tend to be young singles. Historically, Tucson has had difficulty with "brain drain," and while it has a great research university, many who graduate end up moving out of the city. If Tucson can retain more, it means more of the Creative Class stays, translating to more start-up companies, which will bolster the overall economy and could potentially have a tipping point effect.

Place is important for the Creative Class. Cities and the Creative Class come together in somewhat of a symbiotic relationship where each gives to the other the vital nutrients needed with a reciprocal effect strengthening the whole system. Cities need the Creative Class in order to have a strong creative economy and the Creative Class is drawn to the city with all that it offers them.

> The Creative Centers tend to be the economic winners of our age. Not only do they have high concentrations of Creative Class people, but they boast high concentrations of creative economic outcomes, in the form of innovations and high-tech industry growth. They also show strong signs of overall regional vitality, such as increases in regional employment and population. The Creative Centers are not thriving for such traditional economic reasons as access to natural resources or transportation routes. Nor are they thriving because their local governments have gone bankrupt giving tax breaks and other incentives to lure business. They are succeeding largely because creative people want to live

43. Florida, *The Rise of the Creative Class*, 291–92.

there. The companies follow the people—or, in many cases, are started by them. Creative Centers provide the integrated eco-system or habitat where all forms of creativity—artistic and cultural, technological and economic—can take root and flourish.[44]

In many ways one could almost be assertive to say that the more hip and progressive a city is the more vibrant their downtown core is (or vice versa) and the stronger the presence of the Creative Class. The Creative Class is drawn simply to places that appeal to them, their interests, and where they want to live. It then is no surprise that cities like Seattle and Portland rank so high on the Creativity Index. Their downtown cores and urban neighborhoods are attractive, there are ample cultural and lifestyle amenities that abound, one can live a relaxed urban lifestyle, outdoor activities are endless and at their doorstep, there are numerous gentrified neighborhoods such as The Pearl or Hawthorne in Portland or Pioneer Square or Belltown in Seattle, and ample universities and jobs that feed the Creative Class. Place is important! Geography is indeed not dead in spite what many claim in light of the effects of globalization.

> Today's key economic factors—talent, innovation, and creativity—are not distributed even across the global economy. They concentrate in specific locations. It's obvious how major new innovations in communications and transportation allow economic activity to spread out all over the world. What's less obvious is the incredible power of what I call the *clustering force*. In today's creative economy, the real source of economic growth comes from the clustering and concentration of talented and productive people. New ideas are generated and our productivity increases when we locate close to one another in cities and regions. The clustering force makes each of us more productive, which in turns makes the place we inhabit much more productive, generating great increases in output and wealth.[45]

What is it about central cities that act as a natural magnet for the Creative Class? The Creative Class is drawn to cities (some more so than others) because of the various factors that they value. "Essentially my theory says that regional economic growth is driven by the location choices of creative people—the holders of creative capital—who prefer

44. Florida, *Cities and the Creative Class*, 70.
45. Florida, *Who's Your City?*, 9.

places that are diverse, tolerant, and open to new ideas."[46] Florida went on to describe numerous key characteristics of place that Creative types were looking for:

1. Thick Labor Markets: When asked about the importance of employment, the people in my interviews and focus groups repeatedly say they are not looking just for a single job but for many employment opportunities.

2. Lifestyle: The people in my focus groups tell me that lifestyle frequently trumps employment when they're choosing where to live.

3. Social Interaction: In his book, *A Great Good Place*,[47] Ray Oldenburg notes the importance of what he calls "third places" in modern society. Third places are neither home nor work—the "first two" place—but venues like coffee shops, bookstores and cafes in which we find less formal acquaintances. According to Oldenburg, these third places comprise "the heart of the community's social vitality" where people "hang out simply for the pleasures of good company and lively conversations." Creative Class people in my focus groups and interviews report that such third places play key roles in making a community attractive.

4. Diversity: People were drawn to places known for diversity of thought and open-mindedness. They actively seek out places for diversity and look for signs of it when evaluating communities. These signs include people of different ethnic groups and races, different ages, different sexual orientations and alternative appearances such as significant body piercings or tattoos.

5. Authenticity—Authenticity comes from several aspects of a community—historic buildings, established neighborhoods, a unique music scene or specific cultural attributes. It comes from the mix—from urban grit alongside renovated buildings, from the commingling of young and old, long-time neighborhood characters and yuppies, fashion models and bag ladies. People in my interviews and focus groups often define "authenticity" as the

---

46. Florida, *The Rise of the Creative Class*, 223.
47. Oldenburg, *A Great Good Place*.

opposite of generic. They equate with being "real," as in a place that has real buildings, real people, real history. An authentic place also offers unique and original experiences. Thus a place full of chain stores, chain restaurants and nightclubs is not authentic.

6. Identity: The combination of where we live and what we do has come to replace who we work for as a main element of identity.

7. Quality of Place: It refers to the unique set of characteristics that define a place and make it attractive. Generally, one can think of quality of place as having three dimensions: *What's there*: the combination of the built environment and the natural environment; a proper setting for pursuit of creative lives. *Who's there*: the diverse kinds of people, interacting and providing cues that anyone can plug into and make a life in that community. *What's going on*: the vibrancy of street life, café culture, arts, music and people engaging in outdoor activities—altogether a lot of active, exciting, creative endeavors. [48]

Based upon that last point alone it is no surprise that each of my focus cities rank in the top 11 percent of all U.S. cities on the Creativity Index. What they each share in common is that they are in mountainous regions. Denver has the Rockies, Albuquerque has the Sandia Mountains, Tucson has the Santa Catalina Mountains, Phoenix has South Mountain, the White Tanks, and Camelback, Portland has Mt. Hood, Seattle has Mt. Rainier and the Cascades, and Vancouver has the Coast Mountain Range. Each city offers endless outdoor amenities that the Creative Class is drawn to.

Cities are central to the Creative Class. This factor explains why I cannot look at issues like the geography of church planting, gentrification, downtown cores, and not also look at the Creative Class. Florida argues that many cities' revitalization and gentrification are actually driven by the Creative Class who are going back into urban areas. "But urban centers have long been crucibles for innovation and creativity. Now they are coming back. Their turnaround is driven in large measure by the attitudes and location choices of the Creative Class."[49] So if it is indeed the Creative Class who is pouring back into the cities and aiding in the revitalization

48. Florida, *The Rise of the Creative Class*, 223–32.
49. Ibid., 286.

and gentrification process, why? Why the push to go back to the city for many?

> Several forces have combined to bring people and economic activ-
> ity back to urban areas. First, crime is down and cities are safer.
> Second, cities have become the prime location for the creative
> lifestyle and the new amenities that go with it. Third, cities are
> benefiting from powerful demographic shifts. With fewer people
> living as married couples and more staying single longer, urban
> areas serve as lifestyle centers and as mating markets for single
> people. Fourth, cities have reemerged as centers of creativity and
> incubators of innovation. High-tech companies and other creative
> endeavors continue to sprout in urban neighborhoods that we
> once written off, in cities from New York to Chicago to Boston.
> Fifth, the current round of urban revitalization is giving rise to
> serious tensions between established neighborhood residents and
> newer, more affluent people moving in. Finally, in one of the most
> ironic twists in recent memory, both sprawling cities and tradi-
> tional suburbs are seeking to emulate elements of urban life.[50]

Cities are indeed great magnets for the Creative Class. An understanding of this group of people is essential when looking at church
planting in central cities and urban neighborhoods since the city is where
many of them live. They are shaping and influencing cities and this factor
will have a reciprocal effect on church planting and how it differs in these
contexts compared with suburban settings.

These are but a few introductory perspectives on the geography of
church planting and some of the pertinent issues at hand. In order to
understand where churches are being planted and even why, it is essential
to take a step back to see what kind of grand story is unfolding in our cities. It is best to view the city as something living and organic rather than
a mechanistic system of concrete, glass, and steel. The city is continuously
in motion with people moving in while others are moving out. There are
economic, cultural, social, political, and architectural forces at hand that
does indeed shape the scope of church planting. Too often, as Christians
we can so focus so much on the demographics in a city that we miss the
larger picture. While it is vital to know who lives where, their ethnicity,
language group, average age and so on, there is more to the puzzle. It
makes sense why we focus on the human element, especially as church

---

50. Ibid., 287–90.

planters, because our lives are dedicated to seeing the Gospel become a reality in people's lives as they are transformed from darkness to light. We are in the people business. On the other hand we do admittedly have blind spots. What is shaping, forming, and influencing those we're planting among? What economic forces are at play in their lives? How does the global economy impact them? Why did they move to your part of the city where you're planting a church? What influenced them? Are they moving away from somewhere or moving to? Are they part of the Creative Class? As the ideas in the book are brought forth you'll develop a better framework of understanding the city as well as where churches are being planting and why, along with the implications of planting in neighborhoods and districts previously discussed in this chapter. But first, let us take a look at some theology.

2

# Biblical Foundations

Planting churches requires a proper framework regardless if the context is urban, suburban, rural, small city, large city, global mega-city, developed country, or developing country. In some regards church planting is the combination of pastoring a church along with starting up a business from scratch. It is still a unique way of cultural engagement that causes one to do a lot of soul-searching, seeking God, and parsing through personal motives. Why am I planting a church? Am I simply a disgruntled youth pastor looking to make a clean break from the established church to have freedom to do my own thing? Do I find the music style at my current church antiquated thus driving me to create something where I can worship God with cool hip music and, of course, drink lattes at the same time? Am I consumed with following God's heart for the city? Am I consumed with following God period? Do people far from God drive me to plant and I feel my heart rate quicken as I think of seeing new people coming to faith in Christ? What are my motives? Is this simply a good career change and move or am I guided by something else?

This book is a synthesis of numerous topics spanning church planting in general, the study of cities from a 30,000 foot view, an initial foray into a theology of the city, the missional thrust of church planting, and the church as God's agent for social transformation. Church planting must begin with God first and what he says and communicates to us through Scripture. If we fail to realize where church planting fits into God's overall story it can easily be reduced to simply applying the best business techniques and practices. Church planting then becomes a bottom line business amassing numbers, managing and growing budgets, organizational charts, marketing, and the like. In this chapter I will give an overarching whirlwind tour of Scripture. There are four facets of the biblical and theological basis that lay the groundwork for this book: 1) a missional ecclesiology that is highly adaptive for central city contexts and the Creative Class, 2) uncovering a theology of the city to understand God's heart for the city, 3) church planting and God's plan for humanity from the beginning of time, and 4) the church as God's agent for community or societal transformation.

## MISSIONAL ECCLESIOLOGY

It has been said that God is a missionary God and every act since the beginning of time is a missionary act. God is actively pursuing mankind; one can follow this thread throughout the Old Testament, across the pages of the New Testament on to today. God told Abram that all of the nations would be blessed though him. "Now the LORD said to Abram, 'Go from your country and your kindred and your father's house to the land that I will show you. And I will make of you a great nation, and I will bless you and make your name great, so that you will be a blessing. I will bless those who bless you, and him who dishonors you I will curse, and in you all the families of the earth shall be blessed.'"[1] God would use Abram as a building block to create a nation that would be a channel of blessing from God to the whole world. Throughout the ensuing centuries this new nation, Israel, struggled greatly to live out this calling as they continuously fell into sin and away from God. A cursory reading through the prophetic books reveals God's heart to woo his people back to him using numerous tactics ranging from discipline, to captivity, and to simply petitioning them. Israel continued their downward spiral. The prophet Hosea records God's loving tenderness towards his wayward people and his longing to bring them back to himself.

> When Israel was a child, I loved him, and out of Egypt I called my son. The more they were called, the more they went away; they kept sacrificing to the Baals and burning offerings to idols. Yet it was I who taught Ephraim to walk; I took them up by their arms, but they did not know that I healed them. I led them with cords of kindness, with the bands of love, and I became to them as one who eases the yoke on their jaws, and I bent down to them and fed them.[2]

1. Genesis 12:1–3.
2. Hosea 11:1–4.

At the end of the Old Testament times, for four hundred years, Israel did not hear from God, and as a nation they were subjugated under numerous conquering nations. However, God broke the silence and did so in a completely unexpected way. God came to earth as flesh and blood in the form of baby formed in the womb of a teenager.

> Now the birth of Jesus Christ took place in this way. When his mother Mary had been betrothed to Joseph, before they came together she was found to be with child from the Holy Spirit. And her husband Joseph, being a just man and unwilling to put her to shame, resolved to divorce her quietly. But as he considered these things, behold, an angel of the Lord appeared to him in a dream, saying, "Joseph, son of David, do not fear to take Mary as your wife, for that which is conceived in her is from the Holy Spirit. She will bear a son, and you shall call his name Jesus, for he will save his people from their sins."[3]

After growing up and launching out on his earthly ministry, Jesus, at the end of his time on earth, explained to his disciples that as the Father sent him so he now sends his disciples. "Jesus said to them again, 'Peace be with you. As the Father has sent me, even so I am sending you.'"[4] Jesus was the Sent One of God. His mission on earth was redeeming mankind, preaching the Kingdom of God and forming a "new people" to continue his mission. This new grouping of people called the "sent ones" (the church) are now on this same mission that Jesus was one . . . proclaiming the Good News of the Kingdom of God as Jesus tells them just before he ascended to heaven.

> And Jesus came and said to them, "All authority in heaven and on earth has been given to me. Go therefore and make disciples of all nations, baptizing them in the name of the Father and of the Son and of the Holy Spirit, teaching them to observe all that I have commanded you. And behold, I am with you always, to the end of the age."[5]

Like Israel, the church is to be God's channel of blessing to all the nations. This act of blessing is the church's mission. What happens in the

3. Matthew 1:18–21.
4. John 20:21.
5. Matthew 28:18–20.

New Testament with the Great Commission really is an outflow of what took place in Genesis 12.

> This call to Abram shows God's desire for Israel to become a movement that would touch the entire world, not merely a regional organization. God's desire was to bless "all the peoples on the earth" through Abram. God's design for the future of Abram's race is one that was intended to transcend the socio-economic and ethnic borders of Israel. Abram's obedience to God, after many generations, transforms itself into a nation of Israelites. This same obedience, taken on by Jesus' disciples, will again transform itself into today's Christian. God intended from the beginning – his call to Abram – for his Spirit to flow out of the nation into every nation on the earth, Israel, the nation that grew out of Abram's lineage, was to be the prototype of the Church. Genesis 12:1–3 stands as the foundation upon which the Great Commission rests.[6]

The church is only functioning at its highest capacity when it is continuing in the mission that Jesus sent them on. This mission is the core essence of a missional ecclesiology. The way a church exists, structures itself, and operates is as a group of people on Jesus' mission, in other words, being missional. Church is a result of mission and not the other way around. Although it may sounds like mere semantics the implications are enormous.

> By my reading of scriptures, ecclesiology is the most fluid of the doctrines. The church is a dynamic cultural expression of the people of God in any given place. Worship style, social dynamics, liturgical expressions must result from the process of contextualizing the gospel in any given culture. Church must follow mission . . . We engage first in incarnational mission, and the church, so to speak, comes out the back of it.[7]

The mission of the church, this missional ecclesiology, all started back in Genesis 12. The church's existence and what it does is an outflow of the incarnational mission that Jesus sets forth in John 20:21.

> We have come to see that mission is not merely an activity of the church. Rather, mission is the result of God's initiative, rooted in God's purpose to restore and heal creation. "Mission" means "sending," and it is the central biblical theme describing the purpose

6. Gray and Short, *Planting Fast-Growing Churches*, 32.

7. *Hirsch*, 143–44.

of God's action in human history. God's mission began with the call of Israel to receive God's blessings in order to be a blessing to the nations. God's mission unfolded in the history of God's people across the centuries recorded in Scripture, and it reached its revelatory climax in the incarnation of God's work of salvation in Jesus ministering, crucified, and resurrected. God's mission continued then in the sending of the Spirit to call forth and empower the church as the witness to God's good news in Jesus Christ.[8]

This idea is essential, specifically when talking about planting churches in the central city in gentrified neighborhoods among the Creative Class. Church planters are moving away from the cookie cutter approach to church planting, which is encouraging as this whole idea of living incarnationally continues to take root in the imagination of the church and successive church planters. One of the reasons behind this transitory adaptation is the realization that missions is not something that is done "out there" anymore. The church used to talk in terms that missions or engaging in mission is something missionaries do outside the boundaries of one's own nation. However, with the rapidly growing number of unchurched in North America, as well as cities swelling with international immigrants, has come the stark reality that there is no longer a dichotomy in what the church deems as the "mission field." The mission field is right here and in front of the church. The challenge is that the church is struggling to catch up in this shift in thinking as it holds on to the forms and structures of the past.

> With few exceptions, church in the West is still described in institutional terms; a worship service whereby passive laity sit in a sanctuary listening to a didactic monologue from a professional. Most of what we see today as primarily cosmetic changes expressed in the superficialities of style: music style, clothing style, program style, architectural style. Styles may change, but the systematic structure remains.[9]

This mission field is not bound by geography anymore. I see this reality every day that I walk my boys to school. I see Punjabi Sikhs, Indo-Canadian Hindus, Russians, Chinese, and so many more. In the past I would have had to board a boat or airplane and travel extensively to come in contact with all of these different cultural and ethnic groups. Now, all I

8. Guder and Barrett, *Missional Church*, 4.
9. Campbell and Campbell, *The Way of Jesus*, 101.

have to do is walk two blocks to our elementary school. Only thirty years
ago this neighborhood was predominantly Caucasian, and now today it is
roughly 70 percent "visible minority" with most being foreign born. The
mission field is out the church's front door whether they meet in a house
or some other building. The charge Jesus gave his followers in the first
century still holds true today for his followers two thousand years later.
"But you will receive power when the Holy Spirit has come upon you, and
you will be my witnesses in Jerusalem and in all Judea and Samaria, and
to the end of the earth."[10]

One of the problems Christians battle, in regards to living out a missional ecclesiology, is the success of numerous church plants. The temp-
tation is to blindly apply to any setting what these church planters did
in their setting regardless if they are two thousand miles away and in a
context completely different. That approach is lazy missiology and ecclesiology, and void of the grunt work of doing exegesis on the community.
A missional ecclesiology is truly contextual, as Guder explained.

> A missional ecclesiology is contextual. Every ecclesiology is devel-
> oped within a particular cultural context. There is but one way to
> be the church, and that is incarnationally, within a specific concrete
> setting. The gospel is always translated into a culture, and God's
> people are formed in that culture in response to the translated and
> Spirit-empowered Word. All ecclesiologies function relative to
> their context. Their truth and faithfulness are related both to the
> gospel they proclaim and to witness they foster in every culture.[11]

Given the unique nature of rapidly changing cities, a missional ecclesiology is a must if church planters are to engage their community
incarnationally.

> To build on a biblical theme, if the gospel is the seed of God's
> powerful work in our lives and world, then the culture is the soil
> into which it is planted. Therefore, before doing any ministry, a
> missional church first examines the culture, or proverbial soil, in
> which they seek to have the gospel take root. A missional church
> goes to great lengths to understand the people God has sent them
> to. It seeks to know the culture and people better than any other

---

10. Acts 1:8.

11. Guder and Barrett, *Missional Church*, 11.

organization, even businesses, so that Jesus can be more effectively, persuasively, and winsomely introduced.[12]

This missional ecclesiology flows out of what God promised to Abram in Genesis 12 which Jesus continued to keep in front of his disciples as he shares in John 20:21, Matthew 28:18–20, and Acts 1:8.

## THEOLOGY OF THE CITY

If the focus of this book, as far as geography, is the city, then it would be helpful to know what God thinks of the city or whether it is even valued by him. Globally, the pace of urbanization is accelerating rapidly, and for the first time in human history half of Earth's inhabitants live in cities now. If one holds to the belief that God is sovereign and in control, then one must conclude that he is urbanizing the world. In Scripture cities are a prominent topic throughout both the Old and New Testaments. "Indeed the more than 1200 references to cities are but a starting point for discovering God's urban agenda."[13] Cities are a high priority to God, and if he's drawing billions of people to them, then it should be time for the church to take notice. Since God is behind this massive migration then it would make sense to develop urban strategies to compliment what is taking place. However, city life is by nature very complex. "Pluralism in urban life, by definition, quickly brings city dwellers into contact with different values and points of view."[14]

Maybe the question to start with regards the nature of cities. Did cities "just happen" as part of the natural evolution of people or was God somehow behind it all like a great puppeteer above the fray pulling strings and orchestrating the grand story? One of the oldest accounts in all of history regarding the creation of cities is actually found in the book of Genesis. Its beginning is a little murky and leaves more questions than answers.

Adam and Eve had two sons; Cain and Abel. Abel was a shepherd and Cain was a farmer. Like typical brothers jealousy played a part in their relationship, but what was not typical was Cain's response. Abel and Cain both brought offerings to the Lord. "In the course of time Cain brought to the LORD an offering of the fruit of the ground, and Abel also brought

12. Driscoll and Breshears, *Vintage Church*, 223–24.

13. Conn, *Planting and Growing Urban Churches*, 80.

14. Ibid., 143.

of the firstborn of his flock and of their fat portions. And the LORD had regard for Abel and his offering, but for Cain and his offering he had no regard. So Cain was very angry, and his face fell."[15] Even so, God offers him a second chance to make it right. "The LORD said to Cain, 'Why are you angry, and why has your face fallen? If you do well, will you not be accepted? And if you do not do well, sin is crouching at the door. Its desire is for you, but you must rule over it.'"[16] Instead Cain gave in to his anger and killed his brother Abel out in the field.

As a result, God drove Cain away and told him that he would be a restless wanderer on the earth. This is key because what happens next gets a little confusing. To recap thus far, Cain kills his brother and God drives him from the land and tells him he will be a wanderer. Naturally, Cain fears for his own life and that someone would avenge Abel. "Then the LORD said to him, 'Not so! If anyone kills Cain, vengeance shall be taken on him sevenfold.' And the LORD put a mark on Cain, lest any who found him should attack him. Then Cain went away from the presence of the LORD and settled in the land of Nod, east of Eden."[17]

Here's where the tension comes in regarding the founding of cities because of what transpires afterwards. "Cain knew his wife, and she conceived and bore Enoch. When he built a city, he called the name of the city after the name of his son, Enoch."[18] Why is Cain building a city an issue? God sent Cain out from the land and told him he'd be a wanderer, but instead he settled down and built a city.

When God told Cain he'd be a restless wanderer, was that a curse that told of the way Cain was supposed to live the rest of his days as a nomad? Was he to be a wanderer in a literal sense or was this referring to another way? Would he be restless in that he'd forever feel the burden of guilt for killing his brother and be tormented by it?

Was he a wanderer in that he was driven from the ground and not tied to agriculture like he had been previously as a farmer? Did the wandering mean that he could no longer farm and receive his livelihood from the ground? Or did wandering simply mean he was no longer welcome

15. Genesis 4:3–5.

16. Genesis 4:6–7.

17. Genesis 4:15–16.

18. Genesis 4:17.

"home" where God was and where Adam and Eve settled down after they were kicked out of Eden?

Not only that, but another related issue is that of protection and trusting God. When Cain was told that he was sent from the ground and to be a restless wanderer his immediate reaction was that he feared for his life. He didn't want to leave God's presence and to be open to attack. "Cain said to the LORD, 'My punishment is greater than I can bear. Behold, you have driven me today away from the ground, and from your face I shall be hidden. I shall be a fugitive and a wanderer on the earth, and whoever finds me will kill me.' Then the LORD said to him, 'Not so! If anyone kills Cain, vengeance shall be taken on him sevenfold.' And the LORD put a mark on Cain, lest any who found him should attack him.'"[19]

What is interesting to note is that even though he had gravely sinned he still longed for God's presence, which says much about God's nature and who he is. Cain feared for his life and didn't want to be away from God's presence. God reassured him that he would indeed protect him. The author of Genesis then records that Cain went out and built a city. Now, did he do so for reasons of fear that he didn't trust God's protection so he built a city to protect himself? Was the first city created simply out of sin, doubt, and self-protection while not trusting God or since Cain wasn't able to derive a living from the ground his logical next step was to build a city to earn a living, was he simply be resourceful and wise?

The way one answers these questions will have a direct bearing on how he or she views cities. Was the creation of the first city a result of a curse, or was it the result of God's grace and offering of second chances? If it was conceived in sin then how does that affect what Christians or God thinks of the city? Does it? Was it something conceived in sin that God would have to redeem and use it for his eternal purposes? Or was the city God's means of protection? Was the creation of the city Enoch part of God's promise of protection? If so, then one can make the argument that cities were created as a means of grace and second chances for God's protection of his people.

Cities are not inherently evil; otherwise it would seem silly that God would incorporate them into eternity. As Ray Bakke has repeatedly stated, "While the story of the Bible started in the garden it ends in the city." From the very beginning of humankind, the whole trajectory has

---

19. Genesis 4:13–15.

been from rural to urban. Humankind started off as a rural people, yet today over half now live in cities around the world. Someday as God-worshippers we will all live in the New Jerusalem, a city of unfathomable proportions and elegance. If cities were truly evil, then why would we live in one for all of eternity?

> And he carried me away in the Spirit to a great, high mountain, and showed me the holy city Jerusalem coming down out of heaven from God, having the glory of God, its radiance like a most rare jewel, like a jasper, clear as crystal. It had a great, high wall, with twelve gates, and at the gates twelve angels, and on the gates the names of the twelve tribes of the sons of Israel were inscribed—on the east three gates, on the north three gates, on the south three gates, and on the west three gates. And the wall of the city had twelve foundations, and on them were the twelve names of the twelve apostles of the Lamb.
>
> And the one who spoke with me had a measuring rod of gold to measure the city and its gates and walls. The city lies foursquare, its length the same as its width. And he measured the city with his rod, 12,000 stadia. Its length and width and height are equal. He also measured its wall, 144 cubits by human measurement, which is also an angel's measurement. The wall was built of jasper, while the city was pure gold, clear as glass. The foundations of the wall of the city were adorned with every kind of jewel. The first was jasper, the second sapphire, the third agate, the fourth emerald, the fifth onyx, the sixth carnelian, the seventh chrysolite, the eighth beryl, the ninth topaz, the tenth chrysoprase, the eleventh jacinth, the twelfth amethyst. And the twelve gates were twelve pearls, each of the gates made of a single pearl, and the street of the city was pure gold, transparent as glass.
>
> And I saw no temple in the city, for its temple is the Lord God the Almighty and the Lamb. And the city has no need of sun or moon to shine on it, for the glory of God gives it light, and its lamp is the Lamb. By its light will the nations walk, and the kings of the earth will bring their glory into it, and its gates will never be shut by day—and there will be no night there. They will bring into it the glory and the honor of the nations. But nothing unclean will ever enter it, nor anyone who does what is detestable or false, but only those who are written in the Lamb's book of life.[20]

A theology of the city begins with the very first city, found in Genesis 4. The way in which Christians view cities has direct bearing on the way we

20. Revelation 21:10–27.

engage them and the people who live within. Are cities simply sin-cursed locales, or was their whole intention to be a place of grace, protection, and second chances? A proper theology of the city must take into account the formation of the first city, the trajectory of mankind throughout Scripture and history, and the future reality of the greatest city, the New Jerusalem.

## CHURCH PLANTING

The biblical and theological basis for church planting flows out of the first part of this chapter on missional ecclesiology. Without a proper understanding of the mission Jesus calls us to we cannot understand church planting. Church planting is an overflow of living lives as sent ones, which leads to questions about the first "sent ones." Were the early apostles, like Paul, church planters or evangelists? Is there even a distinction? Church planting in Paul's context in the first century looked like the following: he would go from city to city proclaiming the Good News of the Kingdom as an evangelist (one who proclaims the Good News). When people responded to his message and became followers of Jesus the Messiah, then Paul would gather them and a church was birthed. What is a church to begin with? Is the way it is defined today congruent with the first century notion of it? "The word church is a poor translation of the word ekklesia since it implies a sacred building, or temple. A more accurate translation would be 'assembly' because the term ekklesia was used to refer to a group of people who had been called out to a meeting."[21]

This definition is a great link to the idea of missional. The Father sent Jesus on a mission to the earth to proclaim the Good News of the Kingdom. Jesus then sends his followers who are gathered or assembled for a specific reason or calling (the mission!), to go throughout the world proclaiming this same Good News. Church planting is the on-going process of proclaiming the Kingdom of God and then gathering or assembling the people who respond. This process is seen in Acts 2. At Pentecost when the Holy Spirit came upon the disciples in the upper room, Peter began proclaiming Jesus, "But Peter, standing with the eleven, lifted up his voice and addressed them: 'Men of Judea and all who dwell in Jerusalem, let this be known to you, and give ear to my words.'"[22] He then went on

21. McCallum and DeLashmutt, "What Is the Universal Church?"

22. Acts 2:14.

to talk about Jesus the Messiah. What happened next was that the people responded and in a similar context a church was birthed.

> Now when they heard this they were cut to the heart, and said to Peter and the rest of the apostles, "Brothers, what shall we do?" And Peter said to them, "Repent and be baptized every one of you in the name of Jesus Christ for the forgiveness of your sins, and you will receive the gift of the Holy Spirit. For the promise is for you and for your children and for all who are far off, everyone whom the Lord our God calls to himself." And with many other words he bore witness and continued to exhort them, saying, "Save yourselves from this crooked generation." So those who received his word were baptized, and there were added that day about three thousand souls.[23]

Very quickly these new followers of Jesus the Messiah began to loosely function like how we think of church. They gathered regularly for teaching and fellowship.

> And they devoted themselves to the apostles' teaching and the fellowship, to the breaking of bread and the prayers. And awe came upon every soul, and many wonders and signs were being done through the apostles. And all who believed were together and had all things in common. And they were selling their possessions and belongings and distributing the proceeds to all, as any had need. And day by day, attending the temple together and breaking bread in their homes, they received their food with glad and generous hearts, praising God and having favor with all the people. And the Lord added to their number day by day those who were being saved.[24]

There is little doubt the idea of church has come under fire of late, especially within the camp of fellow Evangelicals. Many are seeking to redefine church and, in their attempts, have thrown out the proverbial baby with the bath water or are downplaying the gatherings altogether. Some have even gone as far as to say the church is simply a human conception, and they do not see how it plays into the overall story of God. The church is still vital today.

> Its purpose is to offer salvation, wholeness, healing, and transformation to a sin-sick world. The local church is the only hope

23. Acts 2:37–41.
24. Acts 2:42–47.

humanity has of finding forgiveness and proper standing before a holy and righteous God. Without the Church, the world has no hope. If you do not believe that, then is no use in planting any churches. Close shop, go home, and forget you ever considered planting a church in the first place.[25]

The church is not the Kingdom of God, although the Kingdom of God is present in the church. Therefore, church planting can be viewed as practically expanding the "felt presence" of the Kingdom of God, which is more than simply getting souls into heaven. "This tension of the kingdom being already present in the church but yet not fully unveiled until the return of Jesus allows us to labor in hope until he returns by working on both the spiritual and physical needs of people, caring for the whole person including their food, water, shelter, education, and clothing."[26]

New churches continue on the mission that Jesus sent them on to proclaim the Good News of Jesus the Messiah and his Kingdom. Whether the setting is suburban, urban, or rural, these new churches are best functioning when they do so as indigenous expressions. "Indigenous church planting is sowing the Gospel seed in the native context of thought and things, allowing the Holy Spirit to do His work in His own time and way."[27]

## THE CHURCH AS GOD'S AGENT FOR SOCIETAL TRANSFORMATION

Everything flows out of the initial biblical and theological basis of the mission of God as it was seen in the previous section on church planting. My intention is not to set forth a detailed work on a missional theology. There are numerous books on the subject that handle it in a much more thorough and detailed manner. The mission sets the trajectory for everything else to come. God sent his son Jesus, who then in turn sent out his disciples.

When God was establishing the guidelines for the new nation he created (Israel) and how they were to live and function, he always had a heart for the least, the last, and the lost. All people living under the umbrella of Israel were to be taken care of whether they were a free person

---

25. Gray and Short, *Planting Fast-Growing Churches*, 31.

26. Driscoll and Breshears, *Vintage Church*, 61.

27. Brock, *Indigenous Church Planting*, 89.

or a servant. Even those who fell into debt or servitude were forgiven and freed every seven years. Those who could not work would be taken care of. The Israelites were to give their tithe (ten percent from the increase of their land) to the Levites, strangers, orphans, and widows. God's heart was for the wellness of the whole person.

During New Testament times Jesus pays particular attention to the marginalized. He healed many and was a friend of sinners. Even in his Sermon on the Mount he gave preferential treatment to the distressed, the poor, the hurt, the broken, and the needy. Following in his footsteps, the early church, as recorded in Acts 2, sold their earthly possession to ensure there was no one in need. The early church picked up where the nation of Israel left off in regards to their preferential treatment of the needy, the poor, widows, and the marginalized. Just like Israel was to care for all of those under its care so was the church, and they embodied this immediately. "And all who believed were together and had all things in common. And they were selling their possessions and belongings and distributing the proceeds to all, as any had need."

It is no surprise then that throughout the rest of church history the church has been a catalyst for societal transformation, whether it was through starting hospitals, orphanages and schools; caring for the sick, homeless, or addicts; and the myriad of other ways the church has engaged society. However, in the early twentieth century there was a phenomenon called "the Great Reversal." Simply put, this was the great divorce between evangelism and social concern. Evangelicals moved to the proclamation evangelism side, and those deemed as "liberals" were linked on the social concern side. "Seizing upon some of Rauschenbusch's theological distortion of the kingdom of God, fundamentalists found it convenient to throw the biblical baby of justice and compassion out with the bath water of liberalism. In the process they were as guilty of twisted theology and biblical reductionism as were the liberals; both reduced the gospel to less than what it was meant to be."[28] Prior to that shift the church in America and England was well known for social involvement.

As the church in the West is waking up to the implications of a whole gospel, there is renewed interest in social issues. Just like Israel in the Old Testament, Jesus' earthly ministry, the New Testament church, and the church throughout the past two thousand years, new churches being

28. Conn, *Planting and Growing Urban Churches*, 97.

started today have the opportunity to continue to demonstrate in word and deed God's heart for all of humanity including the least, the last, and the lost. Church planting in urban settings provides an opportunity to see the whole gospel lived out and proclaimed in word and deed.

> At a time of unprecedented global urbanization, the issue of *where* we live out our witness has enormous consequences. Grand strategies to evangelize the world via mega-gatherings and satellite and other state-of-the-art communication methods may have their place. But the task of redeeming our cities will be accomplished on the ground, one block at a time, by courageous people who take the daily risks that bring life to their corner of the world.[29]

Churches that are started in central cities and urban neighborhoods have the incredible potential to transform their host community. "It means that when we plant a church that throbs with biblical vitality we introduce into urban life a force of good, for justice and reconciliation."[30]

One of the struggles is the lack of presence of urban Christians to be change agents for societal transformation. "At the heart of these pressures is the growing size of the non-Christian urban population. The growth of urban cities outside of North America and Europe, coupled with nominalism and the erosion of the church in those former centers of Christianity, has created a significant drop in the percentage of urban Christians."[31] However, with most cities going through massive downtown revitalization projects and various neighborhoods gentrifying, more people are moving back into the city. When it comes to church planting, often times it is the church planters who are good demographers, following population shifts. As more people are moving back into the city, it also means as a reciprocal effect that more churches are being planted there as well. Whereas many churches in suburban settings may be involved in social justice issues from afar, these urban church planting pioneers are confronted with this reality each and every day.

One of the realities of suburban life as a generality is that they tend to be more homogeneous in regards to ethnicity as well as socio-economic strata than in the city. What sets the city apart is the great diversity of ethnicity, linguistics, sexual preferences, and religion, as well as a wide

29. Lupton, *Renewing the City*, 223.

30. Conn, *Planting and Growing Urban Churches*, 22.

31. Ibid., 132.

range of socio-economic levels, all living in proximity with one another. Therefore, church planters, in their contexts, are being forced to deal with social justice issues and to come to grips with a gospel that not only transforms individual lives, but also has the power to change social structures and transform neighborhoods.

> Why should we be concerned about addressing felt needs? How does a this-world focus of meeting felt needs fit with the eternal focus of evangelism? Does not such an approach distract us and dilute our ability to win people to Christ? There are at least three reasons why evangelicals should address the felt needs of city-dwellers. To do so (1) provides a point of redemptive connection with those who are spiritually lost, (2) adds credibility to our communication of the gospel, and (3) is commanded by God and demonstrated by Christ.[32]

Social justice issues do indeed go hand in hand with the proclamation of the gospel and the planting of churches. Urban settings are amplifiers of this reality more so than most every other part of a metro area.

> By addressing felt needs of city-dwellers, we connect with them so that they pay attention. Because we touch them at points of reference, our message gains a hearing. Often, in a natural way, their area of needs becomes an avenue for sharing the gospel. Because we have shown caring at the level of temporal need, we are given permission to express caring for their eternal need.[33]

The church is to be God's agent for societal transformation in the same way that Israel was set up to care for all and give preferential treatment of the marginalized, whether poor or widow or orphan or debtor. God's initial promise to Abram was to be a channel of blessing to all of the nations has found its new home in the church. As new churches are being planted they are conduits of this blessing that flows through them into their neighborhoods and community, regardless of whatever social, linguistic, ethnic, religious, or sexual groupings may be present. They are to embody the Good News of Jesus the Messiah and the Kingdom of God both in word and deed.

This way of thinking brings up the issue regarding vision. Part of the church planting training process in most systems, networks, and denomi-

32. Ibid., 94.
33. Ibid., 95.

nations is to come up with a vision for the new church plant. However, maybe the focal point of the vision needs to change? "Each time I asked about life in the neighborhood, the responses seemed to end up on the issue of church. Was there a vision for the community?"[34] Instead of trying to figure out what the vision for our church is, maybe we should seek God's vision for our city and our distinct neighborhood, then build our church plant around that vision and seek to fulfill it.

In a book like this there are numerous streams of influence that not only inform but direct the trajectory of research, as well provide a framework for understanding the data. What is pivotal is the biblical and theological basis which undergirds this research. Christians can and do look at the raw data collected but it is this biblical and theological foundation that acts as a lens to which to interpret things. Looking at various facets, such as a missional ecclesiology, a theology of the city, church planting, and seeing the church as God's agent for societal transformation provides the lens for this project. All of these mix together, which informs church planting in the city with a view towards community transformation. A metrospirituality is not simply about being trendy Christian urban hipsters; it is loving God, being grounded in Scripture and theologically savvy. That provides the foundation for us to engage the city with the gospel in word and deed. However, it cannot simply stop there. This love, passion, trajectory, and motivation ought to drive us to not only love the city but understand it.

34. Lupton, *Renewing the City*, 225.

# 3

# Urban Renaissance

One of the interesting perspectives in the study of cities is the continual cycles they go through. In particular, the older a city is the more numerous these cycles of birth, growth, maturation, decline, decay, and rebirth appear. In the North American context many fail to realize how relatively new these cities truly are. In fact, there are many cities that were birthed and grew during the time of the advent of the automobile. This has enormous implications in the way cities were designed and laid out. Vancouver is one such city with a relatively recent history. Local Vancouver resident and author Matt Hern makes the observation in his book, *Common Ground in a Liquid City*, "This is a young city of ebullient and energetic ascension, with all the attendant naiveté and optimism. This is a city with almost no urban past, and one that seems to believe that every day is going to be sunnier and more profitable than the next."[1] Although metro Vancouver has been densifying around their city centers and boasts of one of the densest downtown cores in North America, it grew with the automobile in mind.

In contrast, other cities, such as Chicago, Montreal, and various European cities were built and developed in their central cities before the rise of automobile. With that in mind, urban planners had to think through issues of ease of access for people as they were on foot or horse. If that is how a typical city dweller got around town there's no trekking six miles to one's "local" Starbucks. These cities were designed to be dense in their cores and mixed-use development was part of the fabric of urban life. Mixed-use development simply means that zoning allowed for residential and commercial use to coexist. What it may look like are residential units sitting atop ground-level commercial businesses. It would

1. Hearn, *Common Ground in a Liquid City*, 40.

also be common to find corner grocery stores in residential neighborhoods. Over time, with suburban sprawl, the two began to separate. The argument was, "I do not want a corner store next to *my* house." In many suburban communities replete with track homes one would have to drive to get to the closest commercial amenities.

While my family and I lived in Tucson, I vividly remember trying to cut down on driving our SUV. Part of it was related to escalating gas prices and the other part was attempting to develop and experiment with a practical theology of creation care. I figured I could love Jesus and honor him by reducing my carbon footprint. From the very beginning, I realized how this was unpractical, inconvenient, and even somewhat undoable in my part of the city. It was a mile to the nearest grocery store, coffee shop, and other amenities. We lived in a typical suburban development with over 500 homes. Every fourth or fifth house looked the same and we were bound by what colors we could paint our home. Uniformity was key. I thought I would be pretty savvy by attempting to live a more sustainable lifestyle, especially in a desert environment where most basic resources do not come easily. The first day I went to our local coffee shop it was over 100 degrees outside, traffic on the "side road" was zipping past me at 55 to 65 miles per hour, and there was no shoulder. By the time I got to the coffee shop I was all sweaty and flustered. It is one thing to bike to the coffee shop but another to get groceries or transport an entire family. Our children's school was three miles away on similar shoulderless roads and the next closest coffee shop and shopping area was four miles in the other direction. Even the nearest bus stop was miles away. Needless to say we continued to drive our gas-guzzling SUV.

What does this have to do with urban renewal or renaissance? Tucson grew and developed like most North American cities. Although the city's roots go back thousands of years, its built environment was and is shaped by the auto. For most of my time in Tucson I moonlighted as a hiking and mountain biking guide. From the beginning of our church planting journey, I realized quickly I was an ineffective fundraiser and, therefore, I had to get a job. Theological education was and is great, but I was not well-equipped to get a job outside of a vocational ministry setting. I did not meet the basic requirements, certification or educational requirements for many jobs I looked at. However, I did see an ad in the newspaper for a hiking and mountain biking guide at a local resort. I sent in my resume, chalked full of vocational ministry experience, as well as theological and biblical education. When I did not hear anything from the resort for a month I assumed I did not get the job. However, one day out of the blue they called me and a few days later I went in for the interview. My "interview" consisted of a two hour hike and then jumping on the tail end of an advanced mountain bike ride. I did get the job and it turned out to be one of the most enjoyable experiences I have ever had.

Every day, as a team of guides, we took guests out into the desert for a hike and then a different group for a mountain bike ride. We were sitting literally on the edge of a trail system that spanned the entire Santa Catalina Mountains. Out the resort's back door we had access to miles of pristine single track trails for hiking and mountain biking that wove through the mountainous foothills in the Sonoran Desert. One of the amazing features of the desert environment is arid climate. Apart from it feeling incredibly refreshing, especially if you are from a humid climate, the dryness has a preserving effect upon local archaeology. Part of our hiking experience was to take the guests through old Hohokam village sites. The Hohokam were aboriginal people who lived in the area from about the time of the birth of Christ right up to the mid-1400s. Most of the remains that we came across were from the latter years of their existence. We found thousands of pieces of pottery shards, numerous mortar and pestles, petroglyphs, and foundation stones from village walls or their pit houses. A walk through the desert is a walk through history. We learned to be pretty adept at finding pottery and other remains on most every hike we led throughout the mountain range. On occasion we would even find sites that the archaeologists for the forest service did not know about.

The name given to these ancient desert dwellers, the Hohokam, was a rough translation simply meaning, "all used up." It was surmised that one of the reasons for their abrupt disappearance was that their villages grew too large and could not sustain themselves in years of drought. They were dependent upon certain streams and rivers that would flow perennially and when these began drying up, coupled with competition with other tribes for resources, they simply packed up, left, or assimilated into other groups. This history defines Tucson today. This is also a parallel of what happens in many cities and neighborhoods, not only in North America, but cities worldwide.

While a whole city may be in continual growth and expansion pattern, there are always distinct neighborhoods and districts going through the process of birth, growth, peak years, decline, and decay. Like the Hohokam, changes occur in a community, whereby many perceive it as no longer sustainable for living and people move out. There has been an identifiable pattern in our cities as neighborhoods decline and people move further out. Neighborhoods that once were vibrant hubs have since fallen on hard times and decay sets in; all used up. Across North America we can trace this phenomenon in city after city, often coupled with the introduction of different ethnic and minority groups into that neighborhood. In the 1950s and 1960s, this took place in vivid fashion as immigrants and minorities continued to pour into the cities. As a result, ethnic Caucasians streamed out to the suburbs in what has been dubbed "White flight." What one ethnic group thought was "all used up" became a new home for another. As the Hohokam moved out of the Tucson basin, other aboriginal groups came in on their heels, as well as the first Europeans in the 1500s. As ethnic Caucasians moved out of urban neighborhoods, other ethnic groups came in on their heels.

Urban renewal, renaissance, or gentrification is a tricky and sticky topic to wrestle with, especially when it comes to living out faith in the city. There are numerous forces and varied issues at hand that makes the process complicated, whether we are referring to affordable housing and the displacement of lower income families, income inequality, or even the positive benefits like historical preservation and retention of a city's character. What happens as neighborhoods gentrify and revitalize is that it launches the whole community into a flowering renaissance of sorts. An area once in serious decay becomes exciting as people move back in and buildings are reclaimed and restored. This has a positive ensuing effect in that the local economy becomes vibrant again as new businesses like boutique shops, coffee shops, and restaurants spring up.

History is replete with this notion of birth, decay, and rebirth. We have a panoramic view of the past hundreds and thousands of years as we take note of civilizations ebbing and flowing like the tide. Ancient cities came and went while others have endured up until the present. Great civilizations and empires, like the Greeks and Romans, had their apexes while their influence continues to be felt. On the other hand, other civilizations, like the Chinese, have been active for thousands of years and continues to do so even gaining great momentum on the global stage. One of the significant moments in relatively recent history, especially in the global church, was the Protestant Reformation. In essence it was a sort of a revitalization or massive gentrification project done on the church. Like an old neighborhood there were signs of decay and neglect. Revitalization came and set forth a new trajectory that the Protestant church has been on ever since.

It is interesting to note what took place leading up to the Reformation. Great movements in history do not happen in a vacuum or simply erupt without any warning. William Estep, in his book *Renaissance and Reformation*,[2] makes the argument that both of these historic events are intricately related. Without the Renaissance there would have been no Reformation. There was a flowering of culture, a rediscovery of the arts that paved the way for the events of the Reformation to take place. The cultural milieu of the time was so stirred up that the ideas of the Reformation had fertile ground in which to germinate and grow. The same can be argued about urban renaissance or renewal. Often times, it has a stirring effect upon those living in neighborhoods. New people are introduced to these communities with new ideas, new businesses, new developments and the spiritual soil becomes fertile for something amazing to happen. This is key for church planting. Church planters in these neighborhoods have a vital role to play.

A neighborhood's renaissance can lead to a spiritual reformation. As these old communities revitalize there is vibrancy that returns, creating a buzz, and even momentum. Pretty soon this movement takes a life of its own where urban renewal is widespread as it reaches a tipping point. Could this be one of the triggers that leads to a spiritual reformation, where people's hearts are open to spiritual issues? As we will explore later on, this renaissance also can have a negative effect on longstanding urban denizens who are part of the working class or service industry. There is a likelihood they chose to live where they did because it was affordable and close to their job. Living and neighborhood conditions may have been less than ideal, but they were close to their jobs and were accessible to public transportation and other urban services that they depend on. Urban renewal can have a devastating effect in that people can easily be priced right out of these ideal locations, even pushed to a city's periphery;

2. Estep, *Renaissance and Reformation*.

housing may be more affordable but the services they desperately need are now too far away and public transit is sporadic.

A key verse that I am beginning to see more frequently on the websites of new church plants is Jeremiah 29:7. "But seek the welfare of the city where I have sent you into exile, and pray to the LORD on its behalf, for in its welfare you will find your welfare." Many are familiar with this passage of Scripture and the story behind it, but let me quickly summarize and review. At this time in Israel's history they had been taken into Babylonian captivity. The sins of the people were too blatant as they continued to live unrepentant lives. God warned them time and time again through the prophets, but the people refused to listen. Finally, God sent in King Nebuchadnezzar of the Babylonians to sack Jerusalem and take the people back as captives and refugees. He left a small remnant behind, but most were either killed or relocated. It is to these exiles in Babylon that the prophet Jeremiah conveys these words of the Lord.

To the Israelite living in captivity, these words had to almost be scandalous to hear. Seek the welfare or peace of Babylon? Their city was sacked, the walls and temple decimated, the people were slaughtered and dragged into a foreign land as the spoils of victory. They were now being held captive against their will and still reeling from images they will never forget of this great war and bloodshed. Images, no doubt, still linger as they drift off to sleep each night. The words from Jeremiah almost sound mocking. Seek the welfare of the city where they are in exile? Bless those who were merciless? Invest in the city and long for its betterment?

This is exactly the role new church planters in gentrifying neighborhoods need to see themselves in. While they are not even remotely close to being an exile they are to seek the welfare and peace of these communities and bless those who live within them. For numerous decades, as urban cores in city after the city across North America declined and decayed, there was a steady stream or migration of people out to the suburbs. Whereas, in the early part of the twentieth century, these same neighborhoods may have been vibrant and healthy over time, through neglect and the city's rapid outward expansion, they became forgotten for the new. Many who grew up in dense urban neighborhoods all of a sudden could afford a slice of the American pie. The American dream became synonymous with the suburban dream where many longed for their own home and a patch of grass.

Like the Reformation, there were numerous factors that shaped issues of suburbanization and the decay of urban neighborhoods. The past two centuries saw cities in Europe and North America become the focal point of the Industrial Revolution. As a result, the very nature of these cities began to morph. Job availability began shifting more prominently to the city where new factories emerged. This spurned on and sped up the rural to urban migration, a migration which reached a frantic pace. Cities continued to grow as people moved in from the rural hinterlands to take up jobs in factories. Numerous social issues cropped up that would plague cities, and even how they were viewed over the ensuing centuries. Any inklings of an anti-urban bias would only exacerbate the deplorable ailments of urban life. In the mind of many, the city began taking on the form of something entirely ungodly. Skylines were dotted with the belching smokestacks of factories and the living conditions of the working class were crowded and unsanitary. Rural was viewed as wholesome and good while urban was akin to the evils of society. "The city was observed through a bipolar moralistic model of rural versus urban. Everything rural was good, everything urban was bad. Urbanism as a way of life was ultimately an acid that would eat away traditional rural values and undermine meaningful relationships and institutions."[3]

This was the view of the city I had growing up in the 1970s and 1980s. Cities were big, dark, crowded, unhealthy, and unsanitary. The dark images, like from Batman's Gotham City, were locked into my imagination. The closest large city where I grew up was Des Moines, Iowa. Hardly a megacity, but to me it was Gotham City incarnate. On the other hand nearby Chicago was so otherworldly that it terrified me.

In one of the great ironies in life I went to college in inner-city Omaha, Nebraska. Like Des Moines, both were cities of under a million, but to me they were right up there with the world's megacities. The college I attended was a mere mile from the downtown core. While in a relatively safe neighborhood I felt as if I moved into a war zone. It seemed dense. I didn't know anyone, and was it a foreign land compared to my small town upbringing. I despised it. I did not understand cities and didn't care to because all of the stereotypes I had growing up were playing in my mind like a broken record. City life was difficult for me to stomach then, but the suburbs become a quiet respite for me. Most often, recreation was found

3. Conn and Ortiz, *Urban Ministry*, 160.

in the suburbs, whether malls, bookstores, or open green spaces. It was there that I told people that I could indeed breathe. Looking back I can now identify that it was my connection with my small town upbringing that made the suburbs an appealing place for me. Within me was housed this anti-urban bias on several fronts. From my rural upbringing cities were viewed as negative. Theologically or biblically, I had no framework in which to think about the city. When I arrived at college in Omaha I had been a Christian for only a year. During my early spiritual formation and bible college experience I do not ever recall hearing about God's plans or design or heart for the city. God was indeed a rural God, as we learned stories of David, sheep, shepherds, and the early Desert Fathers. During my last two years of college I even had aspirations of being a pastor in rural western Nebraska among the ranchers. I recall sitting in a class on rural church ministry thinking how this would be such an ideal life. God has a great sense of humor.

The way the church responded to the industrialization and densification of cities was, at first, reactionary. Whereas in the time of the early church the wilderness was viewed as the dwelling place of Satan and his minions the city in the Industrial Revolution took on that moniker. It was dark, overcrowded, and the antithesis of what it means to be a Christian. "During the first stage of the emerging great cities Christians joined to anti-urban bias towards the city as a place. As early as the 1830s and 1840s, church sentiment in Europe was turning against cities as strongholds of irreligion, as religious deserts. That view quickly took on traditional status: urbanization leads to the decline of faith."[4] This mode of thinking was embraced by many Christians and remains prevalent. Since this epoch the church has been battling with an anti-urban bias and its influences, which I will get into later. I believe it plays a role in the geography of church planting and why most church planters opt for the suburbs. Rather than running from the city a metrospirituality runs towards it and embraces it.

It should be noted that during this era in modern history the whole city was not relegated to being an overcrowded polluted place for each and every urban dweller. While this might have been the plight of many in the working class those with means could and did move further out from the central city. Land was more readily available, open spaces were abundant,

4. Ibid., 161.

and new parks were designated. For example, Forest Park in St. Louis was created in 1876 and was the site of the Louisiana Purchase Exposition in 1904. As an urban park it is 50 percent larger than New York's Central Park.[5] This separation of the affluent and working class continues to be a point of contention today and throughout a city's existence. Those with means can afford greater access to urban amenities and yet live far from any negative conditions that they might be subjected to. With rampant "White flight" in the 1950s and 1960s it hollowed out many neighborhoods in the city. As a result, there arose an enormous disparity between income levels of inner city dwellers and those who could afford to live in better environments. "Income inequality within developed countries has been widespread and significant since the mid 1980s. This has affected most countries, with large increases observed in Canada and Germany. Consequently, social exclusion, urban segregation and persistent pockets of destitution and poverty are increasingly common in cities of developed countries."[6]

To remedy the overcrowded and unhealthy conditions of the industrial city several ideas about a new urban future were brought to light. Some simply call these ideas utopian, but the reality was that with the deplorable conditions many urban dwellers faced these were hopes and dreams for a better future. London-born Ebenezer Howard saw these horrid conditions and slums around the turn of the twentieth century. He wrote down his ideas in a book reprinted in 1902, called, *Garden Cities of To-morrow.*[7] In the face of unsanitary and crowded urban settlements, Howard's idea merged urban and rural together in one metro area. He believed that city dwellers could enjoy all of the benefits of urban life and yet there was to be ample green spaces, fresh air, and natural beauty. He advocated for the creation of these new "garden cities" that were master-planned and surrounded by a green belt of agricultural land. These garden cities became the template for the suburbanization of our cities. Who could argue with that? I believe one of the fears many have of our urban future is that as cities grow and densify they will begin to look more like clips out of *Star Wars* movies with cities being almost exclusively metal, steel, pollution, and no greenery. Certainly, most would find this unap-

---

5. Wikimedia Foundation Inc., "Forest Park."

6. UN-Habitat, *Planning Sustainable Cities*, 31.

7. Wikimedia Foundation, Inc., "Garden Cities of To-morrow."

pealing. Often times, a city's beauty, apart from the built environment, can be found in what is not urban. Chicago has the lakefront, New York has Central Park, Denver sits at the foot of the Rockies, and Los Angeles has the beach and surrounding mountains. Howard envisioned a better urban future where people could enjoy the best that urban and rural had to offer together.

Le Corbusier, born Charles-Édouard Jeanneret-Gris in Switzerland, was a French architect, designer, and urbanist. Like Howard, he saw the problems with the living conditions in the city and sought to remedy them. The slums in Paris were the context in which he set forth his ideas for a better future. He surmised that if the working class could be housed in high-density high-rise towers it would free up valuable ground around the base of the towers for green space and open air. "He was a pioneer in studies of modern high design and was dedicated to providing better living conditions for the residents of crowded cities."[8] These ideas were formative for public housing that would span across many of the cities of North America. Hindsight shows that high-density living for the poor is not enough, which later were dubbed the "projects." They became synonymous with substandard living conditions, as well as crime and delinquency. With that said, Le Corbusier did what was right; he attempted to rectify inadequate living conditions for the working class and should be commended for that. Many of today's high-density, compact central cities can attribute their influence to this man.

There were others as well who had ideas of a better urban future. The famous architect, Frank Lloyd Wright, would also dabble in envisioning a better urban future with his Broadacre City. Paolo Soleri, also an architect, set forward his idea of "arcology." "An arcology is a hyperdense city designed to maximize human interaction; maximize access to shared, cost-effective infrastructural services like water and sewage; minimize the use of energy, raw materials and land; reduce waste and environmental pollution; and allow interaction with the surrounding natural environment."[9] Something these four men had in common was that there was something about the city that did not resonate with them. They saw problems, whether crowded living spaces, lack of green places, or slum-like neighborhoods, and, through their influence and design

8. Wikimedia Foundation, Inc., "Le Corbusier."
9. Wikimedia Foundation, Inc., "Paolo Soleri."

ideas, sought to remedy them in the ways they knew how. "'Modern' urban planning emerged in the latter part of the 19th century, largely in response to rapidly growing, chaotic and polluted cities in Western Europe, brought about by the Industrial Revolution."[10] The reason why this trip down memory lane is pertinent to the topic of urban renaissance is that these ideas paved the way for the suburbanization of our cities. If cities were compact, unsanitary, and constricted then it made sense to move outwards where there was ample open space available.

As these ideas took root it did so at a key span in time. This epoch saw the rise of the automobile, which made the suburbs an accessible reality. Along with that came favorable lending conditions after World War II. Pretty soon, with the track home, affordable mortgages, and the proliferation of the auto, suburban life was not only doable, but ideal. This became synonymous with the American Dream. As more people moved out to the suburbs, it had a hollowing effect on many of our cities. New shopping malls and strip malls cropped up further out from the central city. Soon people were not driving back into the city to shop. More businesses followed the migration of people to the suburbs. Freeways took root and expanded, which meant people could live further out from the city. If they did still commute back into the central city it was to an office building and then back home at the end of the day. Cheap oil prices also played a role.

Suburbanization is not some great evil but where one part of the city thrived, other parts fell into disrepair at the continuation of the outward migration. Historic neighborhoods were left to neglect and what once were vibrant communities, in some cases became war zones with escalating poverty, slum-like living conditions, and the rise of crime.

To explore the topic of the geography of church planting there are numerous issues and forces at hand which need exploration. There are no simple answers and interpreting the research can be tricky. In the ensuing chapters of this book I will reveal the study results of where churches are being planted today. I will make the argument now that, as a society, we are still experiencing some of the leftover influences that I brought to light in this chapter whether it was the church's anti-urban bias in particular or utopian visions of a better future that paved the way for the suburbs. Many still view urban life as the way it was thirty to fifty years ago; unsafe,

10. UN-Habitat, *Planning Sustainable Cities*, 10.

crime-infested, overcrowded, and a detriment to one's life and health. That is not the case in many cities now.

To reference a whole continent's urban trajectory is tricky. It is not an apply-all template. There are cities that have always had vibrant urban neighborhoods and while suburbanization did take place it did not hollow out the city. Cities like New York and Chicago have always had vibrant compact central cities while others that I looked at in my focus cities went through this hollowing out phenomenon on various levels. That is not to say Chicago or New York do not have their areas of urban decay, but their central cities survived intact and thrived. The sprawling desert cities of Phoenix, Tucson, and Albuquerque are making attempts to densify and revitalize their cores. Denver, Portland, and Seattle are bastions of hipness and coolness in their central cities now while Vancouver boasts a high-density downtown core with the majority of its skyline consisting of residential towers.

The first time I heard of the term "gentrification" was while I was a church planting strategist in Tucson. I was sitting in a class in Seattle surrounded by urban ministry practitioners and leaders. It was one of those settings where everyone knew what it was and I was the odd man out. So I smiled and nodded along as if I knew exactly what the term was. Sure enough, since I had my laptop computer in front of me I quickly googled the term and found out what it meant. After that day I became keenly interested in the development of Tucson, the gentrification of various neighborhoods, and the city's goal to revitalize the downtown core. I began spending significant time there and in the surrounding areas like Fourth Avenue and Main Gate Square on the edge of the University of Arizona. Tracking the growth and development of the central city, as well as numerous other gentrification projects, became a fascination of mine. During this journey I was introduced to the writings of Richard Florida and his idea of the Creative Class. That launched me on a personal quest to find this Creative Class in Tucson, to see where they lived, and how they were not only shaping the city, but also its future. Eventually, it dawned on me that there was a direct correlation between the presence of the Creative Class and revitalized downtown cores.

Although I have addressed the topic of gentrification already in this book and will continue to do so throughout I feel it is pertinent to take another look at it. Urban renewal, urban renaissance, and gentrification are all part of the same idea. When one looks at the city it is a topic that comes to the forefront in many cities. "Gentrification—the transformation of a working-class or vacant area of the central city into middle-class residential and/or commercial use—is without doubt once of the more popular topics of urban inquiry."[11] As we find ourselves on the front end of the trend to plant churches back in the city this is an issue that needs to be addressed by church planters; often it is the Creative Class who are a part of the early gentrifiers. Gentrification is a double-edged sword as there is a complexity of social issues at hand. Who does a new church plant focus on in these settings? Since I believe that church planters themselves are part of the Creative Class it is only natural that they focus on those like themselves. On the other hand, in these gentrifying neighborhoods, there is still a big gulf between the "haves" and the "have-nots." This will continue to be the case until the transition of the neighborhood is complete and the working class and lower income are pushed out. Until then, the church planter stands with one foot in both worlds: a heart for the Creative Class who are moving into these districts and those who have been there a while. Blue collar and no collar coexisting with white collar.

If we were to pan the camera back we placed on the city and take in the panoramic view of the global city we see this renewal phenomenon taking place all over, but in different ways. It is difficult to talk about urban issues and keep the focus narrowly on the Western world, and North America in particular, although, that is the context of most who will read this book. As cities grow and expand so does their influence. In some ways they are like city-states and wield a lot of influence and power. The top-tiered global cities are all interconnected as we think of New York, London, Paris, and Tokyo. They form a symbiotic relationship in that what happens in one affects the others. Add to that list cities like Los Angeles, Hong Kong, Chicago, Shanghai among others and one begins to see the branding and influencing effect all of these cities have. They not only have relationships with other cities in their region and country, but again, they are interconnected globally. Every city from the top-tier down the list to bottom rung all go through the process of birth, growth, decay, rebirth, and renewal. It simply looks different but gentrification is a global trend. "Gentrification has worked its way into planning manifestos

---

11. Lees, Slater, and Wyly, *Gentrification*, xv.

of urban policy agendas to improve the economic, physical, and social outlook of disinvested central-city locations around the world."[12]

Another difference to take into consideration is whether the city is in a developed country or a developing country. In developed countries many look at the city through the lens of it having poor inner cities and affluent suburbs, while in developing countries the cities are the exact opposite. Urban renewal that takes place in developing countries looks different than in developed countries. The pace of urbanization continues to speed up the burgeoning effect upon cities, felt more acutely in developing cities, which are urbanizing at a much faster rate than their counterparts in developed nations. "A total of 193,107 new city dwellers are added to the world's urban population daily. This translates to 5 million new urban dwellers per month in the developing world and 500,000 in developed countries."[13] The collateral issues at hand are the squatter settlements that rim the urban periphery. In this setting we must ask what urban renewal looks like. The ways that neighborhoods and districts of cities in developed nation were built reflect cultural foundations that have been intact for centuries. Viewing an urban renaissance in cities in developing countries cannot happen by applying the template used by European and North American cities. "The most obvious problem with master planning and urban modernism is that they completely fail to accommodate the way of life of the majority of inhabitants in rapidly growing, largely poor and informal cities, and thus directly contribute to social and spatial marginalization. The possibility that people living in such circumstances could comply with zoning ordinances designed for relatively wealthy European towns is extremely unlikely."[14] Why? They are different contexts and have different needs. What would the role of new church plants in these settings look like? How would people feel if the church only focused on the spiritual and neglected the physical, whether proper sanitation, clean water, and job opportunities? It would almost be scandalous to think of new churches neglecting the physical. To bring this back into the context of cities in the developed world, it is imperative to ask ourselves some of the same questions. When we plant new churches

12. Ibid., xxi.
13. UN-Habitat, *Planning Sustainable Cities*, 26.
14. Ibid., 12.

in urban neighborhoods, do we focus on the spiritual, the physical or both?

Since learning about gentrification it has become quite a fascination of mine to track and study this phenomenon. It has been an astounding journey to follow and note this movement in many cities across the US and Canada. It is more than a hobby, but a passion and a pursuit. When I first visit a new city I immediately make a trek into the central city. For me, the best way to get to know a city is from the inside-out. Start in the downtown core and work outward. When I do this I see traces of gentrification everywhere I go. People are moving back into the city and it has created an urban renaissance in many cities. Church planters are also following people back into the city. Although I would argue that we are still at the front end of that trend there has been more attention placed not only on cities, but on global cities and the proliferation of ideas and conversations regarding city-reaching, city-building, and a mindset shift followed by a population shift of more church planters moving in.

Urban renaissance continues to sweep across the cities of North America. One could argue that cities are continuously in the pattern or birth, growth, decay, and rebirth, renewal, and renaissance. Even in the context of one city, this is going on simultaneously and at a different pace in the varying neighborhoods and districts. New master-planned edges cities continue to crop up, older parts of the city spiral downward while others are finding new life and vibrancy. New church plants have an enormous role in these settings to glue together a community, elevate the social capital, and bring about a spiritual renaissance and reformation where lives are redeemed and communities are transformed as the peace and welfare of the city is sought.

# 4

# The Geography of Church Planting

Research can be a tricky topic. The results can be spun in a number of directions. We do this all of the time in our day to day lives. If I am trying to be financially frugal then spending $30 on a shirt seems a bit much at times when I can get four for the same price at a thrift store, but then again, $30 for a new mountain bike tire is not a bad deal and I feel like I saved money. I would have spent the same amount of money either way. Research and the ensuing data can be viewed the same way.

Recently, I was looking over the notes of an annual meeting for a denomination and there were two numbers that jumped out at me. In the past year as a whole, they saw 27 churches planted. There was indeed much to celebrate as new churches were birthed and even more lives changed. On the other hand, in that same year there were 32 church closures, so in reality they experienced a net loss. What does the research and data say? Is there cause for celebration or remorse? It all depends how you look at the data.

Like I mentioned before, the parameters of my research spanned seven cities in the western half of North America. How applicable is the scope of the results here, especially when one lives in the Midwest, the South, East Coast, or overseas? The reality is everything is data. In the past when I was on assessment teams assessing potential church planters, we repeatedly heard, "Everything is data." With clipboards in hand and just short of wearing white lab coats and hair nets, we would jot notes on everything we saw take place among those being assessed, whether it was during the activities or interviews, sitting down and eating together, or free time interaction. *Everything was data.*

In some ways, I hold up these seven cities as a generic template in which for viewing all other cities but the problems with templates is that they can fit everyone and yet no one at the same time. Templates or models most often are so generic they can be likened to fortune cookies. There is something for everyone, even when my seven year old reads one that promises him financial success in his immediate future. The questions to wrestle through are: Do these results apply to my setting? What can I learn from these tendencies? Is it reflective of my city? How does this cause me to think through issues of the geography of church planting?

The first task I set out to do was to locate and map the gathering place of every church plant I could find within the seven focus cities since the year 2000. I initially planned to use three different church planting networks, organizations, and denominations for all the cities, but quickly learned it was not possible. The reason was that not all of the agencies I looked at had church plants in each of the seven cities. For example, at the time of the research one of the largest networks surveyed had church plants represented in six out of seven cities, but there were some limitations as they had no churches in Tucson, only one in Albuquerque and a candidate planter in Vancouver. On the other hand, they had 18 church plants in the Seattle metro area alone since 2000. Other well-known groups were even less evenly distributed among the focus cities. There were numerous denominations represented in Vancouver with one in particular standing out, which has a very strong church planting network with 13 church plants since 2000. However, they are not planting in any of the other focus cities.

After an internal debate I came to the conclusion not to reference specific church planting networks and denominations in this book, though it might prove helpful to have better context when referring to each city or which groups are leading the charge within. I came to the conclusion that it would end up being a distraction. The goal is to take the pulse of the overall city and to not focus on the strengths or weakness of the varying groups active in church planting. Therefore, I write in generalities when referring to the church planting networks and denominations. This also aids in that I do not claim my lists or research was and is completely exhaustive for each city. With that said, I am very confident I have documented the vast majority of new church plants since 2000 within each of my focus cities. This serves as an ample sampling in which conclusions can be drawn.

## CHURCH PLANT LOCATION AND COMMUNITY TRANSFORMATION SURVEY

The survey was a significant source of data collection for me in this process. I was able to send it out to over two hundred church planters in the seven focus cities. The survey itself went through several updates and changes in order to streamline it for efficiency and ease of data compilation. The goal was to disseminate the survey, asking church planters in the focus cities what the determining factors were for the site selection of their church plants. I wanted to learn from them what they considered as "success." Lastly, I inquired about their involvement in community transformation activities within the district, community, or neighborhood of their church plant.

For those who are planting churches in gentrified neighborhoods among the Creative Class, there was an additional part of the survey. It was critical to be specific on who was to fill out the second section, so I asked for planters who were planting in gentrified neighborhoods and then explained what that meant. I also was curious as to how they were engaging the Creative Class in evangelism, both in word and deed. In order to better aid their understanding of the nature of my inquiry, a description of the Creative Class was given so these church planters, whether familiar with that term or not.

### Creative Class Research

Since a significant element of my research regarded to the Creative Class, I wanted to explore this group of people. In particular, it was essential to spend time defining and explaining who they are, what they do, what they value, where they live, and how this all plays into church planting in cities and, specifically, in gentrified neighborhoods. Also important was to find out what the rank of each in reference to the Creativity Index. For review:

> The Creativity Index is a mix of four equally weighted factors: (1) the Creative Class share the workforce; (2) innovation, measured as patents per capita; (3) high-tech industry, using the Milken Institute's widely accepted Tech Pole Index (which I refer to as the High-Tech Index); and (4) diversity, measured by the Gay Index, a reasonable proxy for an area's openness to different kinds of people and ideas. This composite indicator is a better measure of

a region's underlying creative capabilities than the simple measure of the Creative Class, because it reflects the joint effects of its concentration and of innovative economic outcomes.[1]

This index gave me a better understanding of the state and strength of the Creative Class in each of the studied focus cities. Here is how the cities ranked (with the exception of Vancouver since it is located in Canada):[2]

1. Seattle—#3 overall in Creativity Index Rank (#21 Technology, #15 Talent, #3 Tolerance)

2. Portland—#7 overall in Creativity Index Rank (#12 Technology, #45 Talent, #7 Tolerance)

3. Albuquerque—#11 overall in Creativity Index Rank (#11 Technology, #47 Talent, #37 Tolerance)

4. Denver—#14 overall in Creativity Index Rank (#61 Technology, #18 Talent, #25 Tolerance)

5. Phoenix—#28 overall in Creativity Index Rank (#31 Technology, #75 Talent, #54 Tolerance)

6. Tucson—#32 overall in Creativity Index Rank (#33 Technology, #93 Talent, #50 Tolerance)

8. N/A/—Vancouver BC

*Gentrified Neighborhoods Research*

I am keenly interested in collecting data on gentrified neighborhoods. In each of the focus cities I tried to define and identify the different gentrified districts or neighborhoods where new churches are being planted through the survey I sent to church planters. In it I asked if they were planting a church in a gentrified neighborhood and then asked them to list the name of it. I sought answers from the church planters via the survey about how they are engaged in proclaiming the Gospel to the Creative Class both in word and deed.

1. Florida, *The Rise of the Creative Class*, 244–45.
2. Ibid., 356–57.

*Demographic Statistics*

Lastly, this section is a brief explanation of how and where I collected data about basic city and metropolitan population. For this element of data collection I simply searched the online encyclopedia, Wikipedia, for each of the cities. In it I used their numbers for the city (municipal), as well as for the whole metro area. In instances when I referred to the downtown populations of various cities corresponding references were cited in the footnotes.

The methodology of research was implemented to gather information on where and why new churches have been planted in the seven focus cities in the western United States and Canada since the year 2000. It provided a good basis for collecting data and offered a basic direction for the way the research was to go. In hindsight there are some minor tweaks that I would have changed if I were to do it again, but for the most part, this methodology was beneficial. It was helpful in the sense that I knew where I was going with my research and even why. I was confident in the information gathered, whether it was the demographic studies, the results from the surveys, or researching the intricacies of the Creative Class. There were certainly challenges that the research exposed in the process such as clearly defining gentrified neighborhoods, but overall after a year of collecting data and refining my searches, inquiries, and surveys, I am comfortable with what I found.

## FINDINGS AND RESULTS

Before I launched into gathering data for my research, I developed some hypotheses of which I was eager to test. Based upon exposure to several cities that I was geographically close to and familiar with at the time, as well as knowledge of the general state of church planting in each, I had the hypothesis that most church planting today was indeed done in a suburban context. What makes this hypothesis difficult, as will be noted later on, is defining or putting parameters on what is urban and what is suburban. Do I go by an explicit definition of urban being defined by what is the city proper? For example, in Tucson that definition would mean that roughly 500,000 out of a million people who make up the metro area are classified as urban since they live within the boundaries of the city limits. What makes this definition challenging is distinguishing urban as far as what is in the city limits or by defining a certain density (geography) versus urban as in culture.

Another example would be from the vantage point of where I sat as I wrote this chapter, which was at a Waves Coffee in downtown New Westminster, BC. Although New Westminster is the oldest city in British Columbia and was the first capital of the province, today it is, more or less, considered a suburb of Vancouver. Vancouver acts as the main hub of the metro area with various suburbs radiating out from the center. However, the problem comes with how to define New Westminster or some of the other suburbs. While a city of only sixty thousand residents, the cultural markers would label it as a very urban place. There are two distinct districts, Downtown and Uptown, which are comprised of very compact residential and commercial high-rise cores. As far as central cities or downtowns go, New Westminster has a larger and denser down-town in its built environment than two of the other focus cities in my project. But New Westminster is a suburb, or is it? On the city of New Westminster's website they even classify themselves as urban. When it comes to defining church planting how would I categorize a new church here? Urban? Suburban? Next to New Westminster and sitting in between it and Vancouver proper is Burnaby. Is that a suburb as well? There are four separate city centers, each comprising of compact central business districts full of high-rises. Even the smallest of the city centers has a greater skyline than the downtowns of many larger cities.

What I sought to explore in my research was determining the percentage of new churches that were planted within city limits versus the suburbs. Along with that was another layer of exploration where I was interested in how many churches were planted in the central city or downtown core. Again, that comes with complications as well. What are the agreed upon boundaries of what makes up a downtown core or cen-tral business district? How far out is that boundary extended? As well, in cases like downtown New Westminster, is it classified as urban, suburban, or a downtown core? For the sake of the simplicity I decided to stick with the conventional lines of urban as within the city limits of the main city (i.e. Denver) vs. suburban knowing that it may not always be an indicator of the cultural setting of each church. However, it still shows the trend of where churches have been planted since the year 2000 in the seven focus cities.

*Overall Church Planting at a Glance*

The first task that I tackled was simply compiling the data for where churches were being planted in each of the seven focus cities. In each of the cities I started with several of the larger and more well know church planting networks, organizations, and denominations. Since these entities had websites listing their current church plants, it made my data collection much easier. There was some sifting to do through the various church plants to ensure I only used to the best of my knowledge those started in 2000 or later. Also, I was not interested at this point in churches that had failed, so I only used ones that were still operating and in existence at the time of this writing. In cities where I needed to gather more data, I sought out other and lesser known church planting networks and denominations. In some cases I utilized church plants that were independent as well. This addition was simply for the reason to have more church plants as part of the study. Overall, there were 227 church plants used in this research in the seven cities.

I created a table or spreadsheet where I plugged each church in their respective city. In each city, the first part was to break them down and list them according to the network or denomination that they are a part of. So, for example, under metro Vancouver my first listing for a church planting network was listed alphabetically. I then began listing each church associated with them, which in this case was only one, on my spreadsheet. Then I went to the next network and did likewise. I did this for each city and for each church plant that I had an address for the physical location for their worship gatherings.

Most church plants are part of some kind of denomination or church planting network. For that reason, I searched for these networks in each city through web browsing, asking the various contacts I had in each city, looking at the websites for the denominations and networks since they list their church plants, or contacting the various denominations or networks main office. There were roughly 14 different denominations and church planting networks that I used in collecting data. I felt these various denominations and church planting networks would be indicative of what was happening across the various metro areas. While the list I used was not exhaustive, it does represent the major church planting agencies in each city; therefore, it is a good sampling of church planting in my selected focus cities.

The results break down along several different lines:

1. There is the geography of church planting breakdown in each of the focus cities (urban, suburban, core) (i.e. 3 core, 12 urban, 23 suburban).

2. Within each city, it is broken down into the various church planting networks (CPN) (i.e. CPN #1, 0 core, 1 urban, 2 suburban).

3. There is the overall compilation of the study with all of the results from the seven cities brought together to give the numbers of what is urban, suburban, and core.

4. Lastly, there is compilation of the church planting networks of all the cities and how their numbers breakdown as a whole.

Before I display the results for the overall state of church planting, I will quickly define each of the words used.

1. *Urban*—that which is in the city limits of the city proper (i.e. the city of Seattle rather than the whole metro area.).

2. *Suburban*—the various cities or municipalities clustered around the city proper (i.e. Redmond is a suburb of Seattle).

3. *Core*—the area most commonly referred to as a city's downtown core, city center, or central business district. For sake of defining this category more specifically, this area extended out two to four blocks from each city's downtown cluster of high-rises.

With those definitions in place, here is the overall summary of church planting among the various church planting networks and denominations in the metro areas of Vancouver BC, Seattle, Portland, Phoenix, Tucson, Albuquerque, and Denver. The total number of church plants that came into existence since the year 2000 was 227.

1. Churches planted in the downtown core—17 (7 percent)

2. Churches planted within the city limits (which includes the downtown core which was 17)—76 (33 percent)

3. Churches planted in the suburbs—151 (67 percent)

To help provide a better context for these numbers is to also measure them alongside the city and metro populations. Compiling the populations for each of the seven cities, the overall population is 16,268,873. This number includes urban and suburban alike. Within the overall population the number for the population of the urban areas is 4,967,970 (that which is in the city limits of each respective city or city proper). Set against the backdrop of the metro population the urban population comprises of 30 percent of the total population. Saying it another would be that 70 percent of the combined metro population of the 7 focus cities is suburban or that 11,300,903 out of 16,268,873 people live in the suburbs.

What is interesting to note is how the overall and city proper populations measure up against the geography of where churches are being planted. If the bulk of a metro's population is suburban would it then be prudent to have that reflected in where the majority of church plants are? Roughly 33 percent of churches planted in metro areas were done so within the city limits which includes the downtown core. With 30 percent of a metro's population being within the city limits, then it would appear that based upon where the population is that urban church planting is right on par with suburban church planting or even slightly ahead. Although the sheer numbers of urban church plants (76) is considerably lower than that of their suburban counterpart (151), it matches almost perfectly with where people are actually living. Therefore, does it make sense to have new churches in urban contexts at a higher percentage since the majority of a metro's population lies outside the city limit in the suburbs? In the next section I will go through each city individually to see what the state of church planting is there, as well as at the end to rank them in comparison with one another.

### Church Planting by City

### Vancouver

Vancouver BC has a metro population of 2,116,581, and within the city proper there are 578,041 people living there. Across the city I found and surveyed church planters from five different church planting networks and denominations. All together, there were fifty-two church plants that started since the year 2000 that were included in the study of metro Vancouver.

Of all of the church plants surveyed among the various church planting networks, 6 were located in the rapidly growing downtown core, which made up 11 percent of all church plants. Combining those with urban church plants in the city limits, there were 14 church plants making it 38 percent of total metro area church plants. In comparison to urban church plants, 27 percent of the metro population lives in the city limits of Vancouver. Rounding out the numbers there were 32 suburban church plants, which was 61 percent of the overall church plants. In comparison to the overall church planting numbers for all of the cities combined, Vancouver was right on target with the general percentages, although the church plants in the city limits were proportionally a bit higher than the population percentages. One of the elements of the study that I did include last minute was the population of the downtowns for each city. For this information I used whatever census material that I could find online for the various cities. Sometimes it was simply using zip code demographics, or in certain cities they were clear about the actual downtown population. In Vancouver, according to the 2006 census, there are currently 77,043 people living on the downtown peninsula of Vancouver which is 3.6 percent of the overall population. This downtown population also represents 13 percent of the urban population. For 11 percent of all area church plants to be in that specific but small area would be healthy indeed according to the numbers

Of the five church planting network and denominations about 86 percent of the numbers came from two groups. The largest church planting network had 32 church plants compared to thirteen of the next largest group. Each group had a slight bias in regards to where their church plants were located. Seventy-five percent of the first group's church plants were in a suburban context. Of the remaining 25 percent that were urban with 9 percent were located in the downtown core. Again, what makes Vancouver particularly difficult is their expression of urbanism, which is the most unique among all of the studied focus cities. The term *urban*, both in culture and built environment, is applicable outside the downtown core. This difficulty can be multiplied times over in various other settings across the metro area. However, the numbers of this book stick with the conventional parameters of *urban* and *suburban*. At the end of looking at each of the cities, I will rank them in comparison with one another.

Seattle

Seattle is the second largest metro area in the survey, behind Phoenix. With a population of 3,344,813, there are 602,000 who live within the city limits. There were four primary church planting networks and denominations surveyed in this research. The two largest networks had 28 church plants since the year 2000 in the first group and 18 church plants in the other. Altogether among all of the church planting networks there are 56 church plants studied.

Given that only 18 percent of Seattle's metro area actually lives in the city limits, there were thirteen church plants found within which made up 28.5 percent of all church plants. These appear to be healthy numbers for the state of urban church planting. What was slightly troubling was the small number of church plants in the downtown core among these church planting networks. The two largest groups each had one respective church plant in the downtown. Seattle's downtown population, according to a 2008 census estimate, is at 55,557.[3] This population represents 9 percent of the urban population and 1.6 percent of the overall metro population. With 3 percent of all metro area church plants to be in the downtown core seems to be in proper proportion, even though one could wish there were more.

Eighty-two percent of the metro area's population is located in the suburbs where 71 percent of all of the church plants were located. As a whole, church planting in Seattle is slightly skewed more heavily in favor of the suburbs compared to the seven focus city average. However, given that 82 percent of the metro's population is in the suburbs then this figure makes sense.

Portland

With an area population of 2,159,720, there are 557,706 people who live within the city limits, which comprises of roughly 26 percent of the metro population. The number of church plants found among the various church planting networks and denominations took a significant drop compared to Vancouver and Seattle. There were twenty church plants since the year 2000 among seven different networks. The two largest networks had seven and six church plants respectively.

One of the first questions asked was why was there a drop in church planting in Portland? Was it simply I did not find enough church plants or networks? I used the same process in each city and am well acquainted with a number of church planters as well as network and denominational leaders. Again, to say my list is exhaustive is not true. Instead my focus

---

3. Downtown Seattle Association, "Downtown Seattle Association."

was to find and utilize several major networks that are active in the city as well as others. An interesting observation is that there was an even breakdown in urban versus suburban church planting across the metro area. There were ten church plants in the city limits and ten outside in the suburbs. Also, out of the seven different church planting networks there was only one located in the downtown core. According to Portlandmaps. com, the downtown population is at 10,000, which was based on the 2000 census.[4] The downtown population is 1.8 percent of the urban area's population, and when it comes to the whole metro it represents only .046 percent; therefore, the sole church plant downtown represents 5 percent of all metro area church plants.

## Phoenix

Phoenix stands out among the other focus cities because of the sheer size of the metro area. On average, the size of the other cities within the city limits is about 550,000. Phoenix's city population is three times that size at 1,567,924. For the magnitude of the city and metro area, the number of church planting was rather average in some regards as well as still abnormally small in other ways. There were six different church planting networks and denominations included in the study of Phoenix. Collectively, they have seen 33 churches planted in the metro area since the year 2000. Again, there were two large networks that stood out with one having 11 and the other with 9. Both groups had at least one church in the downtown core, and overall they favored the suburbs. The largest network had 73 percent of their church plants in the suburbs compared to the 78 percent of the second largest network.

Phoenix's downtown population stands at 17,454 according to Downtownphoenix.com.[5] This relatively small populated city center makes up only one percent of the urban population and .04 percent of the metro population. The three church plants located downtown make up 9 percent of all the church plants spread across the metro area. Like all of the downtowns in the focus cities, Phoenix is going through extensive revitalization as well as a push to create a vibrant and compact core. What is interesting to note is that even though Phoenix has the largest urban

---

4. City of Portland, "Portland Maps."
5. Downtown Phoenix Partnership, "Downtown Phoenix."

population, its suburbs make up of 63 percent of the population and that 85 percent of all studied church plants are in the suburbs there.

## Tucson

Tucson was an interesting case study for me. Of all the cities it was the one that I was the most familiar with having lived there. Because of that asset I had a good grasp of the state of church planting overall in the metro area, knowing who is there and who is not. This greatly aided in collecting data on church plants since 2000. One of the difficulties is that as a whole there is not a whole lot of church planting taking place in Tucson. In every other city it was easy to gathering data from various church planting networks and denominations. Apart from the largest network which had half of the 18 church plants in Tucson, the rest were filled in with loosely affiliated church plants. Tucson is the only city where no other network or denomination, outside the largest one, had more than one church plant at the time of the research. As a result I had to include a few more church plants that might even have been their organization's only church plant west of the Rocky Mountains.

Another point of contention is the lack of church planting found in the downtown core. A one mile radius beginning in the center of the downtown includes 12,704 people, yet there is not one church plant there. Tucson is still on the front end of downtown revitalization with more residential development and redevelopment taking place. One possibility is that church planting follows where development takes place as is observed in suburban settings. Church planters as a whole know, understand, and follow population trends. While downtown Tucson's population makes up only two percent of the urban and one percent of the metro population, there is still a great hole in the central city in regards to the number of church plants.

Tucson's urban population outweighs the overall metro population as it comprises of 53 percent of the share of city dwellers. The leading church planting network mirrors this well in that 55 percent of their church plants are in the city limits as well. Overall, 44 percent of all church plants included in this research were in urban Tucson.

## Albuquerque

There are a lot of similarities between Tucson and Albuquerque. Both cities are roughly the same size and both on the smaller end of populations for the focus cities. They share a heavily Hispanic and American Southwest cultural influence; their downtowns are going through revitalization projects at varying levels and paces; and both are also on the low end of the number of church plants taking place across their metros.

The largest network led the church plants with 9 out of the 16. Just like Tucson, in order to accumulate enough church plants for the study it involved utilizing a number of smaller and lesser known church planting networks. The second largest network had two church plants themselves. Also, Albuquerque was an anomaly in that 62.5% of the church plants found among the studied church planting networks and denominations were actually in the city limits. That left 37.5 percent of the other church plants as suburban. On the other hand, this finding fits the trend for how the city's population is dispersed. Within the city limits lives 62 percent of the population, whereas the rest (32 percent) live in the suburbs. Therefore, church planting is a great reflection in accordance to the way the population is distributed.

Albuquerque's downtown core has 21,575 living in that zip code. In reality, that zip code does extend beyond the downtown core. This zip code comprises of 4 percent of the urban and 2.5 percent of the metro population. At the time of this writing only one church plant was found in the city center among the various church planting organizations and denominations.

## Denver

Denver boasts of the tenth largest business district in the United States. What stands out is that there were more church plants found in downtown Denver as far as percentage of the overall metro area church plants at 13 percent than the other focus cities. The leading church planting network led the way with two church plants in the downtown core, as well as 57 percent of their church plants were in the city limits. In comparison, overall 68 percent of studied church plants were in a suburban context. Given that 76 percent of the metro population resides in the suburbs this figure seems to be right on target. With 24 percent of the metro population living in the city limits of Denver and finding that 32 percent of the overall church plants taking place there seemed consistent.

Missing from the study on Denver was the lack of data from the one of the largest networks. Having led the way in each of the other cities, I was not able to obtain information on church planting in Denver during my research process. With that said, apart from the largest network, the second largest church planting network or denomination studied had 12 church plants across the metro area. With Denver having 2,500,000 people in the metro area, it ranked as average as far as number of church plants found compared to the other cities of like size like Vancouver and Portland. Knowing that, the church plants surveyed were merely representatives of a larger whole, though it is difficult to come to solid conclusions about how the cities rank in accordance with one another. If it is by sheer number than smaller cities like Albuquerque and Tucson would be lagging behind or if it is based on per capita, then larger cities like Phoenix would be not fare well.

Table 1. Focus cities at a glance

| City | Church Plants by Location | Percentage of Church Plants by Location |
|---|---|---|
| Vancouver | 6—Core<br>14—City<br>32—Suburban<br>52 total | 11% Core<br>38% Urban<br>61% Suburban<br><br>Population Breakdown<br><br>Core—77,043<br>City—578,041 (27%)<br>Metro—2,116,581 (73%) |
| Seattle | 2—Core<br>11—City<br>43—Suburban<br>56 total | 3% Core<br>28.5% Urban<br>71% Suburban<br><br>Population Breakdown<br><br>Core—55,557<br>City—602,000 (18%)<br>Metro—3,344,813 (82%) |

| Portland | 1—Core<br>9—City<br>10—Suburban<br>20 total | 5% Core<br>50% Urban<br>50% Suburban |
|---|---|---|
| | | Population Breakdown |
| | | Core—10,000<br>City—557,706 (26%)<br>Metro—2,159,720 (74%) |
| Phoenix | 3—Core<br>2—City<br>28—Suburban<br>33 total | 9% Core<br>15% Urban<br>85% Suburban |
| | | Population Breakdown |
| | | Core—17,454<br>City 1,567,924 (27%)<br>Metro 4,281,900 (63%) |
| Tucson | 0—Core<br>8—City<br>10—Suburban<br>18 total | 0% Core<br>44% Urban<br>54% Suburban |
| | | Population Breakdown |
| | | Core—12,704<br>City—541,811 (53%)<br>Metro—1,023,320 (47%) |
| Albuquerque | 1—Core<br>9—City<br>6—Suburban<br>16 total | 6% Core<br>62.5% Urban<br>37.5% Suburban |
| | | Population Breakdown |
| | | Core—21,575<br>City—521,999 (62%)<br>Metro—845,913 (38%) |

| Denver | 4—Core 6—City 21—Suburban 31 total | 13% Core 32% Urban 68% Suburban |
|---|---|---|
| | | Population Breakdown |
| | | Core—10,000 City—598,707 (24%) Metro 2,506,626 (76% suburban) |
| Totals | 17-59-151 (227) | |

### *Church Plants Surveyed Per Capita*

Looking at the sheer number of church plants per city is not necessarily the most accurate way to tell the overall health for church planting in each city. Since there is a great discrepancy of populations between the smallest focus city of Albuquerque with 845,000 people and the largest in Phoenix with roughly 4,300,000 people, a different measurement tool must be utilized. Also, there is the recognition that the list of church plants in each city is not exhaustive. However, the studied church plants from mostly the same networks in each city will reveal a good barometer of the state of church planting. For example, it is easier to assess this data based alone upon the two largest church planting networks surveyed. To my knowledge, what is shown for both networks in each city is indeed an exhaustive list or at least close. This begs the questions: In the largest network why are there 32 in Vancouver but only 9 in Phoenix, which has double the population of Vancouver? Why is the second largest network strong in some cities but non-existent or weak as far as numbers in such places as Tucson and Albuquerque?

Listed below is the breakdown of the state of church planting in each city based on the number of church plants surveyed per capita. Rather than looking at simply the overall number of church plants per city, this format may just be a more accurate reflection of the health, or lack thereof, of church planting in each city. I listed them below based upon ranking from the strongest city down to the weakest.

1. Vancouver—1 church plant per 40,703 people

2. Albuquerque—1 church plant per 52,869 people

3. Tucson—1 church plant per 56,851 people

4. Seattle—1 church plant per 59,728 people

5. Denver—1 church plant per 80,858 people

6. Portland—1 church plant per 107,986 people

7. Phoenix—1 church plant per 129,754 people

This is simply another way to look at church planting as a whole in each of the studied metro areas. This does not paint the entire picture of church planting in a particular city but it serves as another measurement tool in which to view cities. There are many stories taking place of church planting networks forming and growing and in 10 to 15 years there could very well be a different story of each city. In some ways, this may be reflective of the patterns and cycles cities themselves go through: birth, growth, maturation, and decline. There are many in each city who labor in prayer and work over their city planting, growing, and multiplying churches. Some cities may even be nearing a tipping point where church planting could move from addition to explosive multiplication.

### Interpretation

So what do we do with this raw data? It's one thing to have all of this information and data sitting in front of us like a bucket of overturned Legos, but another to begin assembling the pieces into a coherent forward-moving trajectory. Like I had mentioned at the beginning of this chapter, there is the issue of the viability of applying this data widely and in varying contexts. With this we run the risk of the information resembling a horoscope where it can apply to everyone and yet no one at the same time. However, I would like to make the case that results of what I collected are reflective of the overall state of church planting across much of North America.

If you were to see this data as a template of sorts and lay it across your city how would it measure up? I made the argument, and the information backed it up, that the vast majority of church planting does indeed take place in the suburbs. As I conducted informal surveys of other cities in various parts of North America the results were always the same whether

I am talking about St. Louis, Chicago, Toronto, Atlanta, and so on. Again, the question is what do we do with this data? In the remainder of this chapter I will discuss some of the implications of this, what it means, and how it affects church planting.

The first point is that the suburbs are the new urban frontier. This is the growth edge of most metropolitan areas. In the seven focus cities that I looked at, the population of the city proper was most often smaller than the overall metro population with the average size, apart from Phoenix, about 550,000. What that means is that as cities swell with new growth from the process of urbanization, in order to accommodate this, the city most often expands outwards. Cities represent marked boundaries with a higher density than their suburban counterparts. Therefore, it is often easier and even cheaper to expand outward and build from scratch. The closer to the city's core one is land becomes more of a premium and the prices are higher. New construction or retrofitting older buildings is more expensive in these settings. As a result the population continues to push outwards.

Since the trajectory of a city's population is indeed centrifugal it makes sense to have more church planters starting new works in these growing edge cities. These settings are indeed ripe for new churches to be rooted in since with much change and transition comes more of an openness to the gospel. "A growing city is often more receptive to the gospel than a static or declining one, and edge city in the United States more open that a forty-year-old stable suburb."[6] New communities attract new people whether they're moving out from the city, moving from another city, or coming in from the rural hinterlands. This makes for unique circumstances as change is in the air. Many find their roots to be shaken causing them to be at least more open to spiritual issues than ever before. For church planters this indeed is the right kind of spiritual soil to plant a new church.

In my time of working with church planters I have noted that as a whole they tend to be a savvy group of Christian leaders. They have a good pulse of the culture and track the changes taking place in cities. They are also keenly aware of population shifts which means that they follow where people are moving to whether suburban fringe or even gentrified urban neighborhoods. Church planters most often are trained to

---

6. Conn and Ortiz, *Urban Ministry*, 230.

look for and find ripe conditions to plant new churches and since these are often times found in the suburbs then they are simply being faithful to plant churches in these settings. With the focus being on people, since the majority of the metro's population is indeed suburban, then it makes complete sense that the majority of church planters are there.

The second point, which is related to the first, is regarding homophily and its influence on church planting. In a nutshell, homophily is a sociological term that means "love of the same." "It is the tendency of individuals to associate and bond with similar others."[7] I first came across the word reading a book on the intercultural city. The basic premise, which we especially see played out in metro Vancouver, is that when people first move to a city they look for neighborhoods and communities with people most like themselves. We see the concept played out in our neighborhood here. For various reasons, Edmonds Town Centre is a central hub for new immigrants to western Canada. What happens is that many move to the neighborhood but after six months to a year they move on some other part of the city. Why? Homophily. Often times they find where others from their ethnic or cultural background are and move there. It is simple, straight forward, and very revealing. We like people who are like us and are drawn to them. The greater the cultural distance the greater the challenge. "The culture-distance hypothesis predicts that the greater the perceived gap between cultures, the more difficulties will be experienced in crossing cultural boundaries. The similarity-attraction hypothesis suggests that we are more likely to seek out, enjoy, understand, want to work with, play with, trust, believe, vote for and generally prefer people with whom we share salient characteristics."[8] When I read about this idea the light turned on inside of me. Up until this point there was always a low-level disenfranchisement regarding where I was noticing church planters were moving to. I saw that evident in Tucson which is why I kept asking, "Why is everyone feeling 'called' to the suburbs?"

If the idea of homophily is true then that begins changing everything. Sometimes it takes getting away from your setting to see a broader perspective. My contention that I always struggled with was why so many church planters were opting for the White suburbs. As I collected data from over 200 church planters I noticed a trend. From what I could tell

7. Wikimedia Foundation, Inc., "Homophily."

8. Wood and Landry, *The Intercultural City*, 50.

is that the vast majority of the church planters were indeed Caucasian. I estimate that roughly 80 to 90 percent of the church planters surveyed were Caucasian. Coupling that statistic with homophily and cultural distance factors now we can begin to see why church planters indeed plant churches where they do.

Almost all of the church planters I had worked with while in Tucson were Caucasian. Many had come from different parts of the country to relocate to Tucson to plant a church. If we factor in homophily we can see in their decision-making process that when they were looking for where to plant a church one of the first things most looked for were other people like themselves. This might be represented by the stage of life, socioeconomic strata, cultural values, and so on. Since arriving in Vancouver I have been able to see how this concept works out here as there is a large number of church planters from varying ethnic groups. I see Chinese planting churches among Chinese, Koreans among Koreans, Iranians among Iranians, Caucasian Canadians among Caucasian Canadians, and so on. We do not question or even hesitate when we see this taking place because it makes sense and is very natural.

Looking back on my time in Tucson I have a broader perspective on this issue regarding the geography of church planting. What homophily does is help clarify the geography of church planting in the city. I am not advocating for a blind application of this idea which lets new church planters off the hook of laboring through the difficult process of where to plant a church. This does not mean that church planters ought to only interact and plant churches among their own people and in parts of the city they like. I still have internal conflict over that. In some ways we have bought too far into this notion. I question out loud why there is always a larger amount of church planters in what I call "swank" neighborhoods and districts. Why do all of the hip and trendy neighborhoods, whether urban gentrified or suburban, get a plethora of church planters while less desirable parts of the city get little to none? There are issues and forces at hand that might even be deemed ugly that we need to wrestle with which I will get to later on in the book.

The third way to look at the data from the geography of church planting and begin making interpretations is that there needs to be a different approach. While planting a lot of churches in the suburbs is good for that setting, it still does not get at what is taking place in the city. The best way for impacting and influencing the city is not going to be an outside-in approach but instead an inside-out one. As I have sat through numerous training classes, modules, and seminars on planting churches most seem to have a suburban bias. These systems are not trying to skew people to plant in the suburbs but the overall approach, philosophy, and even strategies appear to be most culturally conducive to a suburban context. Urban environments are simply different than their suburban counterparts. Even suburbs vary greatly from one another in that a brand new edge city suburban development is culturally different than a 40 year old inner ring mature suburb.

There are several ideas all converging on this third point; there needs to an inside-out approach to church planting that starts with the city first, there are cultural differences between the city and the suburbs, and the methodological and philosophical differences between church planting in urban versus suburban contexts are unique. My contention is that if we start with the city first we will still get the suburbs. On the other hand if we start in the suburbs it does not mean we will get the city. Cities are like an enormous centrifuge launching people further and further out. Church planting in the city will indeed impact the suburbs as people often times will eventually move farther out whether for affordable hous-ing, better environments for raising a family (which is to be debated), or more open space. Cities also house the cultural centers of influence that not only shape the metro area, but the region and even the world. These would be strategic locations to start churches whether by a university in an urban neighborhood, a major media outlet, or a shopping district to name a few. Again, all of these raise the issues regarding the geography of church planting and the need for church planters to take this into more serious consideration.

The geography of church planting is very revealing. Where churches are being started across a metro area does indeed say a lot. It informs us what places are up and coming and what places are dying or downtrodden. There are numerous factors that shapes and influences where churches are being planted. I have brought to light only a few and there are many more still out there. I do not believe it is as cut and dry of a simple answer of church planters planting among people most like themselves in parts of the city where they desire most to live. The data is the data and there is no denying where the bulk of church planting is taking place. The difficulty lies not only in how that information is interpreted but more importantly how it is applied.

# 5

# Motives for Site Selection in Church Planting

One of the difficulties in conducting any type of research is moving away from hard data onto that which is more subjective. In the study of church planting across metro areas it is easy to determine where churches are being planted by simply locating their meeting place and plotting it on a map. It is cut and dry for the most part. It may not tell the entire story but at least it begins to weave it together. However, this next section gets into the motives of why church planters decided to plant where they did. How exactly is that determined? Also, it takes an enormous amount of introspection and self-awareness to be able to wade through all of the motives that went into site selection for church planting. As I find myself on the front end of the journey of now planting a second church, I can attest to the difficulty of choosing where exactly to do so. The best way for me to illustrate the difficulty is to peel back the curtain and let you into my own decision making process. In many ways it is a messy and painstaking process with no normative template for everyone to follow. My hope is that my own understandings, fumblings, and methods may shed light on the difficulty of the process.

The first time that I had helped plant a church was in Arizona. I vividly remember driving into Tucson with two other guys who were praying through whether to join me or not. I was living in California at the time but was on a trip to New Mexico interviewing to go on staff at a church outside of Albuquerque. I extended my trip so I could visit Tucson where we were all exploring a church planting possibility. I drove from Albuquerque to Phoenix where I picked these friends up from the airport and then we continued on down to Tucson. I am already getting ahead of myself. How did I even narrow my own site selection down to Tucson of all places in North America and the world? Did I have a map up and simply threw darts to choose? I suppose if I was a good aim I would have planted in Hawai'i.

Surprisingly, it was not that difficult of a decision. Previously my family and I had lived in Phoenix for several years while I was on staff at a church and attending seminary. My wife was originally from the southwest and we both had family in Arizona, New Mexico, and Nevada. Apart from where I grew up in Iowa, it was the most familiar part of the country for me. At the time, we were in northern California and when we talked about church planting we had made the decision to go back to the American Southwest, to the desert. At that point it was not necessarily even a spiritual decision in that we wanted to be back closer to family and in an environment that we were familiar with. *Step one was selecting the region.* Once we narrowed it down to that region we began to prayerfully explore options focusing on Albuquerque, Phoenix, and Tucson. *Step two was choosing a city in that region favoring the larger ones over the smaller ones like Flagstaff, Las Cruces, Santa Fe, and so on.*

Through networking I connected with a church planting strategist in Tucson. From the very first conversation we had on the phone it felt like something resonated. He answered my questions, told me about the vision the association had for Tucson, and even encouraged the ideas I had on church planting at the time. After more conversations and emails over the ensuing weeks I planned a visit to Tucson in conjunction with my trip to Albuquerque. Church planting was enticing and I did not know whether to do so now or later. At the same time, I was weighing through this I was also exploring other opportunities to go on staff at a church which picks up where I started with the story.

While I had only been to Tucson once before it was still a familiar setting being back in the southwest. As the three of us drove from Phoenix to Tucson, we talked and prayed asking God to show us what He wanted and for clarity. We arrived in Tucson and made our way across the city to our hotel. If first impressions were foundational for making decisions we would have turned the car around and drove back to Phoenix. We did not like what we saw of the city. There was no positive vibe or warm feelings that made us say, "Eureka! I found it!" By the time we arrived at the hotel we were dismayed and already questioning why we came. There was this sick feeling in my gut and I did not know what it meant. Was this God? Was it simply my unreliable emotions? Bad food? Were these feelings based upon expectations that I had of the built environment of the city?

While I was familiar with Phoenix, and even though Tucson is an hour and a half away, they are completely different cities. Was I feeling this way because I was simply overly tired from the travel? What was going on?

The church planting strategist met us at the hotel and after some initial time meeting and chatting we set out to explore the city. Based upon who we were and the needs of the city he took us to a few places where he thought would be a good fit for us to plant a church. He talked about Tucson and the need for church planting across the city. The first site he took us to did not resonate at all. We did not "feel" anything and culturally it was not a fit. We simply did not like it. What was about it that we did not like? I do not know if I can pinpoint that even now but we felt and experienced nothing. However, that was all about to change soon. He took us to another site where he shared that he had been praying over for quite some time and even pleading with the Lord to send church planters there. As we crested the hill overlooking the area just as he was telling the story we had that "Eureka" moment.

The "a-ha!" moment is kind of odd when we give it further consideration. How is it quantified or measured? In working with church planters I have seen this experience happen over and over again. Sometimes it is powerful and intense while other times it more subtle like unfolding a map as it continues to expand. I would tell planters that it is also like looking at something out of focus and over time the picture becomes clearer. My experience seemed to be pretty quick and intense. Now, what was that? Emotions? God? God working through my emotions? I am not too sure but my thinking and feelings moved from not wanting to be in Tucson to all of the sudden it was all that I wanted. I could envision myself living there and planting a church. As we explored the area I became even more excited. Looking back, I wonder out loud why I was excited and what resonated. We went house-hunting with the strategist and walked in and out of a number of model homes. I liked what I saw. We were no longer in Tucson but an edge city suburb. It felt like home and even familiar to where we lived in metro Phoenix. Needless to say, we went for it. Several months later we made the move and began the church planting journey in that Tucson suburb.

Looking back we always have 20/20 vision. Navigating God's will is indeed a tricky experience for us and our theological background and underpinnings influence us greatly. For some it is a highly rationalistic process while others it is strictly emotional. For me, it was somewhere in the middle. At that point in my life, I still had an aversion for cities and so the closest I could handle was, indeed, a suburb. Urban life still scared me, which explains why I felt angst by driving across the city and staying at a hotel there. Once I got out to the suburbs I felt I could breathe. Whatever took place was enough to get us to clean out our savings account and move to this new city. What was interesting was that after we launched we ended up moving the church out of that suburb. We had aspirations of planting a church for suburban families but most of all who came were college students. That began a slow migration. The church eventually moved from suburban to urban, where it was a few blocks from the downtown core and a few blocks in the other direction from the University of Arizona. I still scratch my head when I think about it all.

As Christians, the decision making process, not only for church planting but for life decisions, becomes more complex in some ways because there is a factor in the equation—God. On the surface it sounds like with God in the picture it should make the decision making process easier, but in many ways our desire to follow him in obedience causes us to scrutinize the details all the more so. How exactly do we make decisions? Is it bottom line weighing the factors like what will pay us the most? What is the best career move? What kind of place will make us or our spouse happy? What city has the best career or educational opportunities? What place makes us feel alive? Where is the greatest need (both real and perceived)? What is good for my family? Are we staying close to family or moving away from family? Do we stay in the area close where we grew up or relocate to a different region or even country? On top of that we always ask: What does God want for my life? There are numerous ideas and theories about determining God's will. How do we decide and what guides our thinking?

These are crucial questions when it comes to site selection for church planting. It goes beyond simply emotions or on the other end crunching numbers. Some make the argument that we ought to make decisions based upon what we see in Scripture. It seems as though we cannot do anything unless we feel "called" to it by God whether it is sitting on some obscure church committee to deciding whether we are going to pray for someone regularly or not. We end up reading our current theological assumptions back into Scripture. The reality is what we assume normative was not so in Scripture. We fail to realize that what we hold is a collection of God's revelation to mankind that spanned thousands of years. In that time frame empires rose and fell, numerous cities were at their apexes only to become wastelands, and countless people who loved and worshiped God lived and died. Yes, God communicated directly and audibly to many, but again, it was over thousands of years and to a select few. Given the scope of Scripture and the multitude of people who worshipped God this audible calling was not normative. Most of us cannot claim God has spoken to us audibly although some can. I am not here to enter into a debate about signs, wonders, cessation of gifts, and so on. What I am trying to communicate is this: most often when it comes to making decisions, both major and small, we most often do not hear God's audible words on the subject. If we did, we would not have to talk about motives and the issue simply becomes about obedience.

If we do not *hear* God's audible voice then how do we choose where to plant a church? While God's audible voice may not be normative on a regular basis for most who're trekking into church planting there still has to be a way to discern God's will and leadership in our lives. The tricky part comes when we attempt to reduce it to an equation or an exercise of logic and preference. On this issue I speak out of both sides of my mouth because, on one hand I believe it is an intuitive process as we listen for God's leading through various means, and yet at the same time, we try and make decisions based upon other factors like gifting, background and upbringing, preferences, geography, and what resonates with us.

I think back in college, sitting in a class taught by Dr. Stanley Udd at Grace University in Omaha, Nebraska. The course was on the Minor Prophets and I knew I was in over my head. I honestly do not remember anything from the class apart from two things. The first one was that in my final paper I completely botched my interpretation of the book of Zechariah but Dr. Udd liked my drawing for the cover and had mercy on me. The second thing I recall had nothing to do with the class.

I do not remember how the conversation came up but we got into the discussion concerning God's will and answered prayer. At that point, I had now been a Christian about four years and was still soaking everything in. Dr. Udd said something that continues to stick with me to this day. He said that if we really wanted to know whether God is answering our prayers and leading us then we simply pray with clear specifics but tell no one. He went on to say that when we pray and tell others about it sometimes Christians on their own can make it happen. I understand as the Body of Christ we are to rally around one another and help but do not miss his point. *When we petition God with such clear specifics and he answers, there is no debate as to what happened.* Not too long after that I graduated and decided to put his idea to the test.

After college we made the decision to move to Phoenix where I would begin seminary. In light of what Dr. Udd talked about I came to the conclusion that I wanted to put those ideas into practice. I created a list of very specific things that I began to bring before the Lord on a daily basis. For complete disclosure here is that list. I prayed:

- for very affordable housing,

- for our moving expenses to be covered,

- for me to find a staff position at a church as a youth pastor,

- for a car with air conditioning since we are moving to Arizona,

- and help with seminary tuition.

It was definitely a tall order but what did I have to lose? My desire was simply to know that God was in this with us, but I was not prepared for what would happen next.

After praying several months all of these prayer requests were specifically and fully answered in a two week span. I was utterly shocked, amazed, humbled, and deeply grateful. Out of the blue I contacted a church about a youth ministry opportunity not knowing whether they even had a youth pastor or not or were looking. There was no ad or job posting that I answered but I got a Phoenix area phone book, found their address, and sent them my resume. The pastor called me immediately. I found out their youth pastor just resigned and moved a week ago. They saw my resume and knew it was from the Lord. I flew out, interviewed, and they voted to hire me all in the same visit. Just wait, it gets better! They told me they were going to pay our moving expenses, too. We had family in the area at the time. They had a house there and as well as one in Mexico and were building another in Colorado. Their house in the Phoenix area had no one living in it and was fully furnished. They had asked if we would not mind staying there for free and that they would cover all the utilities. Not only that, but they had a car in the garage they needed us to drive on occasion to make sure it continues to run well–the car had air conditioning! Free house, car with air conditioning, no utilities, and they gave us a credit card to help take care of the house if there was anything we needed to buy for it. Did I mention that out of the entire

Phoenix metropolitan area, which if you have been there before you understand how it is an enormous sprawling city, that the house where we were moving into was less than two miles from the church? Oh, and it had a pool. Lastly, I applied for the seminary and received a scholarship for half of my tuition. I learned a lot about prayer and God's will from that experience.

The last story I would like to share is in regards to our second church plant we are starting here in metro Vancouver. The factors surrounding this decision were much different than any one we have made to date. Again, part of the process is highly emotive and the other aspect was a thorough investigation. Sometimes self disclosure can be frightening. Often times we like to share that which casts us in a good light. We have an image or persona to uphold and we share or reveal only "acceptable flaws." It is akin to sitting in an interview and the interviewer asks you what your weaknesses are. If we are frequently late we are not going to share that so we go with something safe like that we do not know a foreign language. It is not that I am ashamed of how I made decisions, but they become highly personal experiences that we cannot detach ourselves from. As a matter of fact, it is exactly these experiences that form and shape us. So how did we end up in Vancouver back into the whirlwind of church planting?

The genesis of the story actually started back in 1997. While in bible college there was always a steady stream of ministries and missions organizations that came through to recruit students. Some were local, others were national, and many were international in focus. Needless to say, there was a high exposure to what God is doing globally. During one of the chapels an alumni spoke about camp ministry up in southeast Alaska. It sounded exciting and appealing so Katie and I came back to hear more during an evening information meeting. As we continued to learn about the ministry and hear of the needs I turned to Katie and we both said, "Why not?" I cannot say there was much or really any prayer other than we saw a need and decided to jump in to help. That one decision set us on a trajectory that we are still on today.

On a side note, sometimes I believe we spend too much time pondering and praying instead of simply doing. I know that almost sounds heretical but I do not believe we need a special calling to do everything. What would happen if more people simply rolled their sleeves and jumped into the foray of missional engagement?

We continued to make plans and preparations for our summer in Alaska as camp counselors. We raised our funds, bought our plane tickets, and after graduation flew up to Juneau. While the season of camp ministry was exciting as we saw God work and move it was what happened on the final day as we drove into town to get on the plane homeward bound that changed everything. The camp experience we had was amazing and it opened up our eyes to the Pacific Northwest. We fell in love with the area. I was beginning to get into the whole outdoorsy thing while there as our camp was surrounded by snow-capped mountains and glacial-fed rivers, it sat right on a pristine beach tucked in a bay on the Inside Passage. I cannot say that I was a "mountain man" having grown up in Iowa, but I loved the wilderness. Wildlife was everywhere, ranging from whales to sea lions to bears to bald eagles. Some of the camp staff had even shot a bear in the camp so we ate bear sausage for the first time, along with other nearby delicacies including fresh crab and halibut. But I had never seen a live bear in person. Despite all of our treks into the forest and clambering up mountains I did not see a single one. There was lots of scat but no bear. I desperately wanted to see a bear and it was our last day. I had lived in Alaska in the boonies for three months and had not seen a bear yet. I was also wrestling with calling at the time. I had just graduated from college and was wondering what was next. God stirred something up in our hearts while in Alaska.

The journey back into Juneau to catch our flight was like a funeral procession. I did not want to leave. I did not want to head back to the Midwest. The thought of trading in snow-capped mountains and the ocean for soy bean fields and cattle pastures for scenery was nauseating. As we were on the boat riding along the edge of the bay towards the pick-up point where the van waited for us I began praying, "Lord, I want to come back. I love the Pacific Northwest." I then stopped and thought about how I would even know whether God wanted me to come back or not. We wanted to come back already. We loved the region and were able to see different parts of it on the Alaska Marine Highway. I then prayed, "Lord, I know this is silly, but I have not seen a bear the whole time here. If you show me a brown bear on the way back I know this will be a sign that you want us to come back." I quickly put that thought and prayer out of my mind because I thought it was a bit childish. We made it around the bay into the cove to the pick-up point. We loaded our luggage and began the somber drive to Juneau as we were about 40 miles north of the city. About half way back I happened to glance out my window to the right where I saw a brown bear just standing by the road. In my haste I told the driver to stop the van and I jumped out. I stood in bewildered amazement and excitement as I watched the bear lumber across the road. I was speechless.

In our sophisticated spirituality we purport in North America it is easy to begin rationalizing away our experiences. We are raised cultur- ally, and even as Christians, to be highly rationalistic and logical. We are products of Modernity. Was that really God who showed me the brown bear? Come on, there are bears everywhere in Alaska. This was merely a coincidence. How can I make a major life decision based upon seeing a furry four-legged animal? Since that fateful day that bear has haunted my mind as I kept asking what it meant. Were we to go back specifically to that camp in Alaska to do camp ministry? Was the scope larger?

What did happen was that experience opened up my eyes and heart to the Pacific Northwest as I began exploring and seeking out what God wants for us there. Was the bear really a coincidence? Even though in less than a year we moved to Arizona, which is about as opposite as one can get from the Pacific Northwest, the bear experience never left me. Over the years it began intensifying in ways that I cannot describe. Yes, we moved to Phoenix which I believe God clearly led us to do. Yes, we planted a church in Tucson which I believe God led us to do as well. When I became a church planting strategist in Tucson, it was evidently clear that this was what God was leading me to do. So why not the Pacific Northwest yet? At that point in the timeline eight years had elapsed since the bear-spotting event in Alaska but it was still fresh in my mind and haunted my thoughts during the day.

A year after I took on my role as a strategist, the intensity for the northwest continued to grow. I made trips to Seattle and Portland and every time I was in those cities I felt at home like I have never felt before. I could breathe. I was reminded of Alaska from smells of the ocean and tress, as well as the wetter climate. When I decided to pursue a doctorate there was only one city I looked at: Seattle. The brown bear was even influencing where I was to get my doctorate!

I began studying the northwest from afar, the different cities, and for various reasons I was making numerous trips up to the area a year whether it was for school or church planting training events for our Tucson church planters. During this time I explored numerous ministry opportunities in

Seattle, Portland, and even down to San Francisco since it rounds out the tail end of the Pacific Northwest in geography, climate, and culture.

One of the initial courses I took for my doctorate lasted for two weeks in Seattle. Since the focus of the program was on global urban contexts, we spent much time learning about and discussing cities. At one point in one of his lectures Ray Bakke referred to Vancouver BC. He went on to say how in many ways it was a model city with its lack of freeways, diversity, and distinct neighborhoods. I was mesmerized and knew I had to explore this city that was just up the road from Seattle. Since the course was two weeks, there was a free weekend so I spontaneously decided to drive north. I had no idea where I would stay and had only one name as a contact person who was a fellow church planting strategist in Vancouver. Upon arriving in the city I was utterly amazed. It was a completely different world and the city was unlike anything I had ever seen or experienced. I did a whirlwind tour of the city and explored as much as my short time allowed which included a quick jaunt up to Whistler. Vancouver is a different city. I was not prepared for the enormous difference between it and Seattle, whether it is the built environment or the sheer diversity. The city perplexed me.

I packed away this trip and experience in my thinking. Over the ensuing years opportunities would come and go in the northwest but nothing quite grabbed me. There were several false starts in our attempt to move to the northwest, as well, whether in church planting or strategist type opportunities. Finally I began wondering if the brown bear was simply an experience of a young believer at a vulnerable and impressionable time in my life. The more I dismissed it the more I felt unsettled. The pull was strong. We had even begun building a new house south of Tucson. At the height of the market we sold our other home and began building this new one. In many ways it was a dream home; large, more than enough room for our family, and a place we could stay for the rest of our lives. But something happened. I could not go through with it. Three weeks before we were to move in we backed out and were able to get our money back. We had sold our home, got out of the contract of this new one, and were renting month to month. However, we went in the other direction.

I spontaneously decided to take a new ministry opportunity in Illinois. It seemed like a logical move on many fronts as it was a move up the denominational food chain, plus better money for our family and an increase in ministry responsibility. I would oversee all of the campus ministries statewide, as well as church planting for the 35 and under crowd. There was already an amazing team in place and my supervisor was a friend. The move also meant we were to be close to family for the first time in 10 years and our boys could grow up around grandparents. My dad had recently died and it would give us a chance to be close to my mom. In every way it was a great move, fiscally sound, and a smart career choice. But I was miserable.

On the first day of the job I walked into my new office with my new laptop and phone sitting on my desk waiting for me. I sat down in my chair with my new pressed dress slacks and shiny shoes. In Tucson as a strategist I was a shorts and flip-flops guy. As I looked around the room I almost started to cry. What did I just do? Instantly it became like a nightmare but the problem was I could not wake up. It had nothing to do with the people around me because there are top notch and great. I was a fish out of water and the brown bear was almost roaring at me now. Did I just make the biggest mistake of my life? This was early November and by December I had cut out a picture of Vancouver and stuck it on our refrigerator at home. I was in a funk, the boys hated their new school and living in Illinois, and our house gave us the creeps.

Not too long after that I was in Atlanta for a series of meetings for workers across North America who oversee church planting. While there, I knew I had to reconnect with the church planting strategist from Vancouver. We set up a time to meet for breakfast. The night before, as I talked with Katie on the phone, she felt impressed to tell me what she learned that day from her time with God. She had felt that God had spoken to her to tell me that wherever we need to go I have her full support. We had talked about Vancouver and she knew I was miserable but how could we move? The difficulty was that we just got there, our kids were still adjusting to their new school, city, and state and finally, we were close to family. What would they think? Why would I want to walk away from all of that to make the leap of faith to plant a church from scratch in a new city and country? As we talked on the phone I said, "We have to go for it. I can no longer ignore that brown bear. I have to see if it indeed was from the Lord or not. I do not care if we fail miserably. We need to respond in obedience."

To say it was a leap of faith seems now like an understatement. It was a complete free fall. I resigned from a great ministry job, sold a lot of stuff, including one of our vehicles, and moved in with my mom during transition. We had no supporters, whether individuals or churches, at the time. Slowly, one came on board and so did our denomination, but when we set the date to move we had no idea how we would do it. We began praying for $10,000 for moving and settling in expenses. In a miraculous way, that all came in shortly. We drove across the country by faith in a lumbering moving truck, not knowing where we would live or even how much it would take to live in one of the most expensive cities in the world. There were many times on the long stretches of highway where I was in tears praying and wondering what in the world I just did. When driving across the endless sand hills of western Nebraska or amidst the expanses of northern Utah or southern Idaho, the only thing I had were my thoughts, God's presence, our two boys in the cab of the truck with me, and a myriad of country western music stations. To say everything that happened thereafter went smoothly would not be true. As a matter of fact, I felt like we were just entering the gauntlet which began the day we picked up our moving truck.

The truck we rented was complete junk and had more issues than a guest on Dr. Phil, we lost half our mattresses, a dresser, and some other furniture in the move from water damage which none of the extra insurances we had or purchased would cover it. Our car was broken into the first week in the city, only to be broken into three months later. The same car finally had enough and broke down within months and not having the resources to fix it or even insure it we become dependent upon public transit. Katie's health took a serious hit and she has been hospitalized several times. One bad thing after another seemingly came our way. It was and continues to be simply a challenge to live, let alone to think about church planting. But, we are here. We made it. We are alive. God is good. He has a plan. We are humbled to simply follow him, and not only plant a church here, but to plant our lives. We love it here. Our boys have blossomed. Our walk with God has and continues to deepen. We have seen him work and move in ways to surpasses logic. He is with us.

Deciding where to plant a church is no small feat. At times it seems like a logical and rational decision. I have seen guys take a very methodical approach whereby they base the location of where they planted upon research, their personality and the match of the community, and the needs. On the other hand, I have seen other guys who make the decision based wholly on visions from God. As a researcher, to study the motivating factors for church planting site selection becomes problematic. What are the criteria to be used? How do I navigate through those who take a methodical approach versus those who felt God prompt them in a certain direction? Often times I liken God's calling or will to the black box found on passenger jetliners. The whole plane may crash leaving nothing but flaming debris but somehow the black box is always intact. It makes one wonder why they simply do not make the whole plane out of that same material. Often times, when everything around us crashes and burns, it is that calling we cling to.

There is more to the black box analogy. In some ways, it also becomes off limits or untouchable. All we have to do is evoke the "God's call" saying and whatever we are doing cannot be questioned any longer. It is not for me to judge or question disrespectfully someone's calling. Instead, what I want to do is simply ask questions regarding whether we are hearing God clearly or not or even understanding the scope of God's will for us for a specific situation. On one hand, if we claim everything is God's will, then we can be assertive to say that God prefers to start new churches in the Caucasian suburbs all the while leaving broken, neglected, and ethnically diverse parts of the city underchurched. If everyone is equally called by God, then why are all of the hip and trendy districts receiving more church planters than the less desirable ones? What can we do? It is that untouchable black box.

One of the areas of interest in looking at the geography of church planting is to figure out why churches were planted in their specific location. What were the determining factors that led church planters to make the decision on where to start a church? Was it personal preference? Did their church planting network or denomination steer them in a certain direction? Was it based upon need, whether that was in regards to lack of a church presence or a decayed area in need of hope? Was it familiarity whether location or the group of people they were planting among?

I sent out surveys to each church planter for whom I had an email address. There were a number of church planters who did not speak English well, and there were some that I did not have any contact info, including an email address to send the survey to. As a result, I got about a 25 percent response of all the church planters. This information served as a good sampling from all of the seven focus cities. Here were the questions asked on the survey:

1.  What criteria were used to decide where to place a new church?

2. How do you define success in church planting?

3. How is your new church plant involved in community transformation?

Those were the three questions that I had asked everyone in the survey. I was also specifically looking for information regarding church plants in gentrified neighborhoods and among the Creative Class. For those who were in that type of setting there were three more questions asked which I will touch on later.

1. Are you in a gentrified neighborhood?

2. How are you engaging the Creative Class in evangelism both in word and deed?

3. How is planting a church in and among the Creative Class similar/ dissimilar than what takes place in most church plants that you see around?

### Criteria Used to Decide Where to Place a New Church

One of the elements of this research was to figure out and learn why churches were planted where they were. Were the majority of churches planted in the suburbs simply because of familiarity and comfort or was that where the greatest needs lie? Why did planters choose to plant where they did? What would the results reveal?

I allowed church planters to pick the top two reasons for why they decided to plant a new church from a list on the survey. In order to expedite the process and make it more measurable I came up with ten possibilities for them to choose from. Again, they were allowed to choose two. Here were the ten choices:

1. God's call

2. Need/unchurched area

3. Cultural compatibility

4. Denominational/church planting network guidance

5. Familiarity (whether geographic or cultural)

6. Where there was an abundance of families

7. Where there was an abundance of singles

8. New growth area

9. Decayed area in need of help

10. Location within metro area

What is interesting is that the number one response for the determining factor of where these church planters decided to plant a church
was God's call. The survey did not allow me to extrapolate exactly what
they meant nor how they determined how God called them, but 23 percent of the responses were that God called them. In some ways, from a
purely scientific explanation, this detail is the most difficult one to determine. Looking at an area in the city with physical need or that is heavily
unchurched is one thing, or a location with an abundance of singles, or a
decayed area in need of help, but God's call? Those other points are more
easily measured and tangible, but this area is where one enters into the
realm of the mystical and spiritual. All of the other answers could be classified as "external" motivators because one can tangibly see what is going
on. On the other hand, determining God's will is more "internal" as often
times it is sought through intensive prayer, fasting, and reading the Bible,
as well as other things like seeking godly wisdom and mentors, and so
on. It would have been an interesting side-study to learn more about how
these church planters determined what God was saying to them. Needless
to say though, the impression and belief that God was leading was the
number one response among church planters.

Trailing just two points behind at 21 percent was the response that
it was the need or that it was an unchurched area is one of the primary
determining factors for how church planters decided to where to start a
church. Again, I do not have information of how they determined need,
but nonetheless, it was the need or unchurched area that motivated these
church planters. Church planters tend to do well to track people movements and population shifts. Wherever there is new growth, whether
urban gentrified or suburban new frontier, most often one will find a
church planter in this area. They are known to extensively pour over demographic materials in search for where cities are growing in order to
plant their church in the most fertile soil. However, is there an underside
to all of this that the results expose?

Coming in at third on the list, trailing behind number one by five
points and number two by three points, is this answer: cultural compatibility. Eighteen percent of church planters said that one of the primary

motivating factors for determining site selection was that the area or people were culturally compatible with them. What exactly does this mean?
What does it mean that they were looking for a place or people that they
were culturally compatible with? How does this work together with the
top two responses of God's will and need as the reasons why the chose to
plant where they did? Can I speculate or at least attempt?

Since the primary response to what was the determining factor of
site selection for where to plant a church was God's call, does that then
tie into responses number two and number three? Was God's call based
upon the need as well as cultural compatibility? Also are those two answers the same or different? Is the call to plant a church in an area of need
or lack of churches the same as cultural compatibility? What if an area of
need is not culturally compatible? The fourth response might shed light
on this subject as well. Eleven percent of the answers were that familiarity
was a determining factor of where the church was planted. If one begins
analyzing the data, the obvious question becomes, "Is God's will to plant
churches in needy unchurched areas that are culturally compatible and
familiar?"

Maybe an example from my own denomination would help shed
light on this tension. The North American Mission Board helps fund thousands of missionaries across Canada and the United States. Many of these
funded missionaries are, indeed, church planters like myself. Recently, I
saw a map of North America that listed the number of missionaries state
by state and province by province. In Texas there were over 800 funded
North American missionaries/personnel alone. There are roughly twenty
million people who live in Texas. On the other hand, all across the entire country of Canada there are over 30 million inhabitants. How many
North American missionaries/personnel are there funded in Canada?
Roughly one hundred twenty. Canada has 10 million more people than
Texas, yet it has over 700 less funded missionaries. Was it that God's call
was confused with what was culturally compatible and familiar?

Here is how the responses rank:

1.  God's call—23 percent

2.  Need/unchurched area—21 percent

3.  Cultural compatibility—18 percent

4.  Familiarity—11 percent

5. Location within the metro area—11 percent

6. New growth area—7 percent

7. Denominational/church planting network guidance—6 percent

8. Decayed area in need of help—3 percent

9. Where there was an abundance of families—2 percent

10. Where there was an abundance of singles—2 percent

## Defining Success in Church Planting

The next question that the church planter respondents answered was regarding how they define success in church planting. A tricky element is determining what success and failure is within the context of church planting. Is it all about numerical growth and budget numbers? If it is not, then what is it? Can one define it, measure it, and use it as a template to grade all other church plants? It is an essential question to ask for church planters as they plant in the city and how they view what they are doing. Often times, the way they answer the question will determine how they go about church planting, their involvement in the local community, and how they view issues such as community transformation and gentrification.

I came up with seven possible choices for the church planters to respond to. As well, at the end of the answers I listed "other" and gave them the opportunity to write in an answer that I did not have listed if they did not resonate with my answers. Here were the answers that I had listed:

1. Numeric growth whether in worship attendance or people evangelized

2. Financial sustainability/independence

3. Reproduction of new churches

4. People are being disciple

5. Leaders are being developed

6. It is *not* tied to any kind of numeric growth

7. The community/neighborhood has been transformed spiritually as well as socially, physically, and even economically

Apart from those answers there were three fill-ins that church plant-ers had listed:

1. Faithfulness to Jesus' call

2. God's people engaged in mission

3. Success is cultivating a way of life which includes incarnational service, authentic relationship, and growing Christian spirituality within the context of the neighborhood

When the numbers were tallied, there was a clear winner among all of the answers. Receiving 33 percent of the votes was the answer that people being discipled was the best way to determine success in church planting. In comparison, the second highest response received 18 percent of the votes. What is already noticeable is how difficult this answer and some of the others answers are to measure. How does one measure these results? How does one know if people are being discipled? What does it look like? Is there then a template that can be applied that deems some church plants successful and others a failure based upon this definition of success? This logic goes hand in hand with the previous question of what was the determining factor of how church planters decided to where to plant a church. While saying God's will is accurate and true, it simply is hard to measure. Saying that people are being discipled as a definition of success is nebulous at best, but at the same time, it can be the most accurate answer. However, these church planters were simply responding to the answers given.

Jumping down to the third most popular answer was an add-in by some of the church planters themselves. Ten percent of church planters mentioned that faithfulness to Jesus' call was the definition of success. The reason I add this response right here is that it goes hand in hand with what I have been writing about, as well as the first question in the survey. How does one know if someone is truly responding to God's call? It seems so gray at times. Can one point to any particular evidences of responding to God's call? Along with that evidence, if success is defined by people be-ing discipled, again, what does that look like? What does discipleship look like? Is there any universal template that transcends time and cultures? If it is all contextual, then how does one measure whether a church plant is discipling people or not? Lastly, if success is tied to the first two along with the church planter being faithful to Jesus' call then how does one know that? How does one determine if he or she is being faithful to Jesus' call if one cannot verify or invalidate their calling, or if the definition of success is such a gray area that one cannot truly define it as well? This notion becomes problematic indeed. However, the consolation is that followers of God do live in the realm of the mystical and spiritual where everything is not so easily definable. Christians talk and live in terms of angels and demons, God communicating with us, being prompted by the Holy Spirit, and so on.

The second most popular definition of success in church planting, at 19 percent, is that the community or neighborhood has been transformed spiritually, as well as socially, physically, and even economically. While not necessarily easily definable as well, this response is encouraging. What this shows is that church planters are thinking beyond merely the context of their churches. The reason for church planting is not so people can simply gather together to sing songs but instead to proclaim the gospel in word and deed, and as a result people, families, and neighborhoods will be transformed. It would be interesting to see if this response would have been part of church planters' visions thirty to fifty years ago. This idea may be reflective of the change in how Christians view different aspects of theology such as a more refined view of the Kingdom of God.

Here's how the responses rank:

1. People are being disciple—33 percent

2. The community/neighborhood has been transformed  spiritually as well as socially, physically, and even economically—19 percent

3. Faithfulness to Jesus' call—10 percent

4. Reproduction of new churches—10 percent

5. Numeric goal whether in worship attendance or people evangelized—8 percent

6. Leaders are being developed—6 percent

7. Financial sustainability/independence—5 percent

8. It is *not* tied to any kind of numeric goal—4 percent

9. God's people engaged in mission—4 percent

10. Success is cultivating a way of life which includes incarnational service, authentic relationship, and growing Christian spirituality within the context of the neighborhood—1 percent

Determining God's calling can indeed be tricky as evidenced in this chapter. It is highly subjective and more than that is personal and spiritual. There are no templates for figuring out God's will as he communicates to us in a myriad ways. No two stories are alike. I look at my experience in church planting and each way we have planted a church was a different journey. Not only were our methods for planting different, but even the way we went about figuring the where was unique as well. The first time around was heavily influenced by familiarity of moving to the southwest with its proximity to family and having lived there previously. The second time around was the result of seeing a brown bear in Alaska as a confirmation on whether to return to the Pacific Northwest or not. Along the church planting journey, I have met planters who planted in the same city they grew up. They said they could not conceive of planting anywhere else, while others moved across great distances to do so. Each story is unique to the individual.

While I served as a church planting strategist I would tell potential church planters that I am like a match maker. It was my duty to match them up with the part of the city that resonated the most with them, who they were, and how God had wired them. I felt it was the combination of following God's call with using a somewhat rational approach. Most often it was as though they would feel a call in general to move to the city to plant or if they were already there to begin planting, but then we worked together to find a good spot for them. It was my goal to connect them with the part of the city that was most cultural compatible with them. Since almost all of the church planters I worked with in that time span were indeed Caucasian then, it made sense as to the kind of setting they ended up planting in. That was how I ended up planting where I did the first time around and that was exactly opposite the way we are planting this second time.

Maybe it was out of principle since I was in the middle of researching and writing my dissertation, which this book is based on, when we moved to Canada but I knew that we could not go about it the way we did it in Tucson. Instead of finding where there were the most people like me, I wanted to live in and plant in a neighborhood that was wholly not like me and very diverse, which is why Edmonds Town Centre has been a perfect fit for us. We are a minority ethnically and linguistically and we love our community. We love the urban culture coupled with other influences like gentrification, densification, cultural and socio-economic diversity, a walkable neighborhood, and accessibility to the skytrain and public transit. Each planter and each story is truly unique. The point of this chapter was to simply point these out so that there is more to think through and process in the decision of where to plant a church.

From my experience, both as a planter and a strategist, I would make the case that there needs to be more exploration in to the geography of church planting. It seems like many church planters indeed are called to a city whether they already live there and move in from elsewhere. Often times it is as if that calling is rather generic and even vague at first. However, it is the first critical step that sets the planter in a certain trajectory. For me it was a generalized calling to the Pacific Northwest which unfolded and developed as the years moved on. It was as though there were two aspects of this. The first is the mystical element where God communicates to us prompting us in a certain direction. The second is where we explore and flesh out that calling. I looked up and down the northwest focusing on primarily three cities and each had their own appeal. Portland was enticing with its vibrant downtown core and its funky neighborhoods. Seattle drew me in because I love the coffee scene and the city's "metronatural" mindset. However, Vancouver won out because what we really desired was diversity and an international city. Canadian cities are mind-boggling diverse and Vancouver has connections globally, especially to Asia, whether China, India, and so on.

The first part for our calling was a generalized draw to the northwest. Like I mentioned before it became almost like it was haunting me. I could not shake it. I began following different news outlets and even sports teams whether it was the BC Lions of the CFL to the Seattle Seahawks to the Portland Trailblazers to the myriad of northwest college football teams. I was a sponge and soaked it all in as we were in the decision making process. Geography is not dead. It is important. As a matter of fact, where we live is one of the most important decisions in our lives. It affects our educational opportunities, employment possibilities, our friends, social networks and our children's future. More than likely, our children will meet and marry someone from Vancouver and, more than likely, they will be of a different ethnicity. They could very well go to school at a university here. They are growing up in a global village where almost all of their friends were born in another country and speak multiple languages. They are learning at a young age to have friends who are Muslim, Buddhist, Sikh, and Hindu. Place is important! It shapes everything. Church planters should take careful consideration in deciding where to plant knowing that the ramifications are enormous. While some may have a generalized calling to the area or city there are still others who feel specifically led to an exact locale. Go for it. For the others who are sorting through where to not only live in the city but to plant churches let me end this chapter with the following thoughts.

One of the pivotal books in my own thinking and reasoning behind moving to Vancouver was *Who's Your City?* by Richard Florida. I knew where God was leading us to but was not too sure of the exact city or even part of the city. This time around the goal was to plant in an urban setting that was culturally and ethnically diverse. That is what I knew at that point. Since one of the thrusts of this book is to explore the Creative Class I had read just about everything from Florida that I could get my hands on. When I began reading *Who's Your City?* it was one of those moments I found myself so elated and angry at the same time. I was elated because for the first time everything began coming into focus for me and angry because I had not seen it earlier. Like I previously shared, in the interim between Arizona and Vancouver I had taken a ministry job in the Midwest. It seemed like a logical move with much better pay, close to family, cheaper cost of living, and potentially more influence. The brown bear would simply have to wait. We moved across the country with our hearts in our stomach. Arizona had been a great time in our lives and significant in many ways. We were hopeful and also looking forward to this next chapter. The only problem was that this chapter was only a paragraph long.

I knew I wasn't supposed to be there. It was during this time when I was reading *Who's Your City?* which Florida talked about the three most important decisions that we will make in life: what we will do (job, career), with who (spouse), and where. It was the *where* that I was in anguish over. I felt stuck in a small Midwest city and that now old brown bear continued to haunt me. Florida's book was critical in my thinking to finally get me to the tipping point where I could not do anything but go to Vancouver. "The place we choose to live affects every aspect of our being. It can determine the income we earn, the people we meet, the friends we make, the partners we choose, and the options available to our children and families."[1] When I processed Florida's three questions I began prayerfully

1. Florida, *Who's Your City?*, 5–6.

navigating my own life, calling, and how I considered God created me. Part of his book dealt with the overall personality of cities. It is a unique blending together of psychology and urban geography. "Are people happier when they find a community that fits them? What happens when one's personality is different from that of their community?"[2] When I read that it clicked and made sense. I began to think about and look at cities differently. The really do have a personality per se. Think of cities like Los Angeles, New York, Chicago, or Boston and each place has more than its own vibe but a collective personality. Again, this was one of the reasons why Vancouver continued to rise to the top of the list for us.

Not only does each city have its own personality but each part of the city. Each urban neighborhood is unique compared to the next one over and each suburb is different than the next. Church planters who are considering where to plant in the city, whether urban or suburban, ought to consider this. For us it was the need to be in a centralized urban context. As I have mentioned already it is truly a unique neighborhood. Although it is technically not in Vancouver proper it is still urban in its culture and built environment with its density and feel. If there is a generalized calling to a city then the church planter needs to painstakingly work through the where of planting, which is no small feat.

Since moving into Edmonds Town Centre life has been filled with much tension, more than I would have known going in. In many ways, it is so different from who we were that after about six months we thought we might have made a mistake. We had wanted something completely different from who we were in diversity and ethnicity and our neighborhood provides that. As we would venture into different parts other city I would sometimes turn to Katie and say, "Wow, these are our people. They are just like us." After talking about it we then realized how much we were indeed falling in love with our neighborhood. Some areas have that instant "fall in love factor" and for us it has been slow burning and slow growing.

When it comes to motives for site selection for church planting no two stories are alike. It is not a simple process because there is a confluence of numerous issues and factors at hand ranging from upbringing, personality type, family type, education, prior work background and experience, philosophy of life, and even one's theological framework in regards to

2. Ibid., 190.

the city. If a church planter views the city in a negative light, like I used to, then more than likely they will gravitate towards the suburban fringe. Cities confront our deepest biases and reveals who we really are. I see that issue painfully clear here in Surrey, a suburb east of where I live. In this city there has been a large migration of Sikhs from Punjab, India. Most Sikhs wear a turban on their head and have long beards. Many Caucasians, and many Christians, have struggled against, resisted, and even shunned these immigrants who came to Canada like many others for a better life. They assume these men and families are Muslim and then all of the racial profiling sets in. Maybe it should not shock me, but as Christians are we not to love the whole world like God does? In cities we are exposed to such a varied world and it reveals deep inside who we really are.

This chapter reveals the deep tension of how one chooses where to plant a church. For some it is easy and for many others it is a journey. In some instances, it is very clear for church planters not only what city to plant in but even the neighborhood or district of the city. For the rest of the church planters it takes a while to figure it out. The point I am attempting to make here is to stop and reconsider. The first question to ask is: Is God calling me to this part of the city? Is the decision based on preference or fear? Is cultural compatibility and geographic familiarity the most important factor that weighs the heaviest? My fear is that if we church planters only stick to the parts of the city that we like, love, and are full of people just like us then there will be many parts of the city that will continue to be untouched. Is God truly calling most to only plant in suburban settings or chic urban districts? This information is not to persuade one in any particular direction other than to provide more issues to think through. I have experimented with creating some type of assessment tool for church planters to work through that would simply open their eyes up to the geography of church planting. My simple plea is for church planters to listen to God's voice and work in partnership with him to figure out the exact where knowing that he's created each planter and wired them uniquely which can be a good match for the part of the city they will plant their lives in.

# 6

# Community Transformation

Community transformation is truly a dynamic process. One of the difficulties is to clearly identify what the concept means. How do we truly know when a neighborhood or district has been transformed? What markers are in place? Are there any clear indicators? Is the built environment any different? Are there more open spaces for people to enjoy? If more people are transformed by the gospel then how does that play out on a neighborhood level apart from more people connected to a church? Is the local economy stronger? Are more there more business start-ups? Is the high school graduation rate up? Is crime lowered? Has social capital been strengthened? Is there more interaction among different ethnicities? Are prejudices broken down?

Often times we talk about community transformation but we fail to clearly identify what we mean by it. The tension comes in when we see that overall this is a contextualized phenomenon. Community transformation does and should look different neighborhood by neighborhood and city after city. Not only that but it will look vastly different in cities in developed nations versus those in developing nations. There is an enormous discrepancy between a gentrifying urban neighborhood in the US versus a squatter shantytown in Mexico. Community transformation in an affluent suburb will contrast starkly with a mature inner ring suburb. Community transformation will look different in each of these settings.

The focus of church planting continues to evolve with the ebb and flow of the development of the church throughout history and into the future. When I first ventured into church planting, it seemed like everyone was talking about cosmetics as this was on the upswing of the whole Emerging Church conversation. We learned that in order to be cutting edge we needed to turn the lights off, add a bunch of candles, burn incense, wear Rob Bell glasses, own a Mac computer, get a tattoo, and make sure that our musicians on stage have the appropriate amount of spiritual tattoos, body piercings, and ruffled hair. However, while church planters still tend to dress the part, it feels like there has been a decisive shift.

The Emerging Church conversation evolved into the missional mindset which began to change everything. No longer was it purely about style, which many at the time would argue it was not, but about the outward thrust of the church. As the church began seeing itself as the missionary to culture, it adopted a new posture. Part of the shift was also in relation to what was taking place on a larger scale in the culture in North America. Younger generations, and I am not narrowly defining the parameters to the church, began to take on a different mentality. Sure, consumerism was and is still rampant but more and more people are talking about making an impact in the world beyond simply making lots of money.

It would be a blinded purist notion to think that the church is the pacesetter in culture even though many pastors purport that that should be the case. The church has, throughout its history, reacted and adapted to cultural changes. The same is true here. While society as a whole began teetering in this direction, it was not soon thereafter that the church, particularly church plants, followed suit. While there is no decisive date or time to mark this shift when one reads the cultural tea leaves, there is evidence something indeed has shifted. This cultural mentality coupled with the skepticism wrought on by Postmodernism combined with a renewed focus on the Kingdom of God has created ripe conditions for church plants to jump in to community transformation.

## CHURCH PLANT INVOLVEMENT IN COMMUNITY TRANSFORMATION

Since the focus of the research of this book in general is church planting in metropolitan contexts, one of the elements I was curious about was how involved new church plants were in regards to community transformation. Again, drawing from what I referenced at the beginning of the chapter, the whole concept of community transformation can be nebulous. For the research and the surveys, I decided upon a definition found online and went with it to have a point of clarification. The definition of community transformation used for the survey is as follows: a social group of any size whose members reside in a specific locality, share government, and often have a common cultural and historical heritage, which collectively bring about a marked change in their community, as in appearance or character, usually for the better. This notion goes back to a couple of related issues, the purpose of church planting as well as defining what success is. Why are churches planted in the first place? Is it simply to get a bunch of people together in one building on one hour on one day a week to sing songs and listen to someone teach? Since the church is a transformational force, I wanted to see how church plants as a whole were involved in different elements of that in their own contexts.

The question asked in the survey to the church planters was, "How is your new church plant involved in community transformation?" I gave seven different answers for those taking the survey to choose from. Additionally, I gave them the opportunity to write in their own answer if they did not resonate with the answers given. This option was an opportunity for them to explain ways they are involved in community transformation that were not listed in the survey. Here are the seven answers:

1. Relocation into your target area

2. Volunteerism

3. Partnering with existing organizations/the city

4. Creating new organizations/non-profits

5. Meeting tangible/physical needs

6. Being a safe house for hurting people

7. Picking an issue (i.e. Homelessness, sex trafficking, illiteracy, broken families, etc.) and leading your church to invest in helping/ serving

Here are the several add-on responses from various church planters:

1. Creative arts

2. Changing peoples' worldviews

3. Developing meaningful relationships with neighbors

4. Gospel proclamation

As the results were tallied it became clear that the primary way in which new church plants are engaged locally in community transformation is through partnering with existing organizations and/or the city. This response to the survey led the way with 27 percent of all answers. There were three answers clustered together leading the list that in many ways could be viewed as one and the same. The second place vote at 22 percent was meeting tangible/physical needs, and third place was volunteerism at 20 percent. In order to partner with existing organizations or the city, it requires volunteerism, and when that takes place, tangible and physical needs most often are being met. If all of these answers were combined into one and reconfigured, it came out to 68 percent of the answers. In other words, it is clear how new church plants are engaged in community transformation. It means jumping into the community and giving themselves a way to meet needs.

Here's how the results scored:

1. Partnering with existing organizations/the city—27%

2. Meeting tangible/physical needs—22%

3. Volunteerism—20%

4. Picking an issue (i.e. Homelessness, sex trafficking, illiteracy, broken families, etc) and leading your church to invest in helping/serving—9%

5. Being a safe house for hurting people—6%

6. Relocation into your target area—5%

7. Creative arts—3%

8. Creating new organizations/non-profits—2%

9. Developing meaningful relationships with neighbors—2%

10. Gospel proclamation—2%

11. Changing peoples' worldviews—1%

Whenever community transformation coupled with church planting is discussed, there arises a certain amount of tension. Not tension in that these two activities are incompatible but instead: what should be the focus of new churches be? This becomes like the egg and chicken debate. What comes first? Chicken? Egg? Church planting? Community transformation? One of the missing elements of the survey was the failure to ask the church planters how they began. Was the focus to start a church that engages in community transformation or does the church planter with their nucleus or core engage in community transformation activities first and see a church birth out of it? The answer to this question is indeed revealing and sets the course for different terrain depending on which way the question is answered. While it may be a mental activity of differentiating between two similar (and even in some cases synonymous) activities, let us explore this further.

One of the foundational questions that church planters ought to ask themselves is simply, "How do I see myself?" Do people see themselves as church planters or missionaries? The way that question is answered will often times be telling of the focus of their activities. Church planters most often would see the locus of their endeavors as starting a worship gathering. They are called church planters. Their initial funding and end goal would be for them to start some type of gathering for worship and instruction. That becomes the central focus of their energies and involvement in their community. Start a church and grow it. Leaders in this category see themselves as bible teachers, preachers, pastors/shepherds, organizers, administrators, and the like. Again, I am referring to broad and wide sweeping categories and generalizations.

Community transformation may or may not happen. It may not even be on the pastor/planter's radar who pours much time and energy into the gathering. To be honest, this is the litmus test of how most church planters are measured and how often times they are stacked up against one another. In church planting circles, most often those who garner the most attention via the stage at conferences are those who've been successful in this pursuit. They have been able to successfully gather a lot of people together in one place. This is not a criticism but simply a reality. Those who are being funded to start churches, regardless of what they believe comes first, are ultimately measured by this rubric.

As culture in North America becomes further unchurched, dechurched, or never-been-churched, then all of the sudden the rules change. Funding models, labels, and categories that have been in place for decades may now not be applicable. The pervasive church planter mentality might be more conducive to areas in which the majority are disposed to or grew up with some kind of a Judeo-Christian worldview, regardless of how churched or unchurched the people are. Therefore, when "God" is referenced at least most people have a shared root memory of some sort of monotheistic deity. However, as our cities continue to swell with international immigrants from countries without a Judeo-Christian worldview the starting point is several steps back. Much of church planting lore is about making church still relevant for the disenfranchised and unengaged. But what does a church planter do when people are not even disenfranchised to begin with? What if the whole idea of God, Jesus, or church is not even on their radar? While many assume that is not the case in most places in North America, that is simply not true.

Shortly after we moved to Canada I became aware of a college near where we live. I had hung out at the local Waves Coffee enough to see quite a number of young college students reading and studying. Finally I began asking them where they went to school. I was assuming that they were attending Simon Fraser University up on Burnaby Mountain. However, many explained that instead they went to Douglas College, which is just down the hill in New Westminster, about a five minute drive away. I began to explore online information about the college and even walked around on campus. To my knowledge there was not a single campus ministry there of any kind even though the school had 7,000 to 8,000 students in attendance. One day I spontaneously walked into the student union to get information about any existing campus ministries just to make sure there were not any I had missed. Once I found out that there were none I asked about the feasibility of starting one myself from scratch. I was given the green light under a unique dispensation as they were trying to expand and strengthen the campus clubs scene. Sure enough, we had enough students interested and we applied for club status. As I was talking with one of the students who worked at the school and was processing our club paperwork we were figuring out how to fill out the application. She knew we were a newly forming Christian club and one of the questions on the application was in regards to what our club activities would entail. I shrugged my shoulders and asked her what would be appropriate to put down on the application. What she said completely shocked me. She said, "You know, I do not know. I really do not even know anything about Christianity."

Here was a student in her early 20s, tech savvy, and part of the global youth culture but she did not know anything about Christianity! It was not even on her radar. Ethnically, I surmise that her family came from India or possibly the Middle East. She would be deemed a typical college age young adult in Vancouver. It seems that in many other contexts in North America we are dealing with a culture that has been turned off by the church, but what do we do with a culture that was never turned on to it in the first place? They are not disenfranchised because they have never been franchised. They are not apathetically uninterested since they were never interested to begin with. This goes back to the mindset–does a person see themselves as a church planter or a missionary? Like many, I track and follow a myriad of church plants and I find a common theme on their websites. They are out to make church relevant, uplifting, cool, encouraging, appealing, hip, and inspiring whether through music, teaching style, or ambiance. I understand this and there have been thousands who have come to faith in Christ in such churches. Is this the same trajectory of the church planter who instead sees themselves as a missionary?

What is the biggest difference for a leader who sees themselves as a missionary engaging the culture first as opposed to being a church planter? Is there a marked distinction between starting with community transformation first versus planting a church? Again, while it may be akin to splitting hairs, there is an enormous difference between a church planter and a missionary who starts churches. The reality is that much of our church planting activities, particularly in the US, we would not do elsewhere. No one questions that or even resists. Why? Because we understand there is a difference-but is there really a difference? Many surmise that church planters can do one thing here and something completely different in another country. To some degree that is true. It is part of being contextual. The point I am trying to make is that North America is indeed a bone fide mission field, which means we need to reorient our posture that many others of late have written about. It is easy to propose these ideas now and then talk about them over coffee with other church planters, but in reality, it is hard to make the switch especially when funding is attached to numerical expectations.

Just this morning I was having coffee with a church planter on the north shore in North Vancouver. Out of the roughly 200,000 people who live on the north shore he mentioned that on any given weekend there might be upwards of 4,000 people worshipping God together. That is two percent of the population! Is this grounds for a church planter approach or a missionary? What does a missionary do that is a marked difference from a church planter? Obviously I am writing generalities but nevertheless it still is good for discussion's sake. A missionary often times has a different approach in that their immediate goal is not to start a worship service. They spend time enculturating and learning the language and customs of their new host culture as they weave their lives into the fabric of the city and build relationships. The end goal is to proclaim the Gospel, and hopefully, out of that see a church arise. Only this is not church planting in the typical manner that we often speak of today. Why is it that methods done overseas would be scoffed at here and yet we have a long history of doing the reverse where we export our ways of doing and being a church elsewhere?

Now when one is making a case, it is easy to create straw figures that are applicable to everyone and no one at the same time to throw things at. This was my intention to bring up a point. We cannot do church planting the same way we have done it even in this past decade. A new way forward is essential. Somewhere there needs to be a convergence of practices we use natively or in our own country or religion coupled with our methods outside our homeland. This is where community transformation comes in. Far from being a privatized faith, the Gospel has the power to change more than our political allegiances or make us swear or lie less. The ramifications are far reaching! During the course of my research and sending out surveys to various church planters, the questions went through a couple of revisions. I first sent out the survey to church planters with open-ended questions rather than allowing them to check a box out of a list of multiple possibilities. One of the reasons for the change was for ease of data compilation and the other had to do with the kinds of answers I was getting in return. I initially wondered whether my questions were clear or not in regards to what I was looking for but the overall impression I got was troubling.

When it came to questions surrounding the topic of community transformation I received many answers that were nebulous and non-specific. Some church planters shared that their only interaction with the outside world in terms of serving the community or anything related to community transformation was simply that they had a worship service. Others took a step forward to say that the only way they were engaged in community transformation was through proclaiming the Gospel and that it was not about serving or meeting needs but simply telling people how broken they are and how much they need Jesus.

Part of active community transformation is taking and combining the roles of being a typical church planter with a missionary along with realizing the larger picture of the Gospel. I understand that we in the West are the products of the Enlightenment and Modernity which means the elevation of the individual. We talk about our personal quiet times, our own walk with God, personal holiness, and a very privatized and individualized faith. That is and has been part of the Christian culture we are swimming in. As North American cultures races towards a multicultural society, suddenly our view of the Gospel and church come into direct interaction with believers from other cultural worldviews. Given that housed in North America, in particular Canada, are some of the most multi-cultural cities in the world, this interaction continues to shake up the paradigm of how we do and be church and the way in which we view the Gospel.

The Gospel has the power to change everything. A community transformation approach makes the case that the implications of the Gospel are far-reaching and can be evidenced by seeing society changed. For so long the focus was the individual but now we are seeing a bigger picture. The reality is that we can gather lots of people into one place on one day a week to sing, worship, and receive instruction, but have little to no effect in a one mile radius. Earlier in the book I wrote about the church as God's agent for societal transformation. In God's economy from the very beginning it was mandated that there be provisions for the widow, the orphan, the foreigner, the debtor, and the like. God's urban structure was one of justice and equality. His reign was more than people gathering and making sacrifices at the temple. Life as God intended included worship, offerings, and prayer but also caring for the oppressed and the marginalized. Jesus did not skip a beat with this. It was the way Jesus lived.

The good news is that roughly 7 out of 10 church planters were leading their churches to partner with existing organizations and the city, thereby meeting tangible and physical needs, and volunteering their time. This is highly encouraging! The first go around for church planting for me was focused on the weekly gathering. I was just beginning to be exposed to community transformation thinking but, to be honest; it was a back burner issue. The focus was still on the church gathered and how to grow it, which I was not very good at. Sure we painted houses among the Hopi in northern Arizona and served at an orphanage in Naco, Mexico, but I did not think too much about our immediate neighborhood. Some of the things I did could even be considered bait and switch tactics. I know my motives were truly to see people come to faith in Christ, but to me then, the Gospel simply boiled down to people praying a prayer and getting their one-way ticket to heaven punched.

Circling back around to the question I posed earlier, what comes first . . . do we plant a church to engage in community transformation or jump in and serve the community to see a church form out of it? The reality is that we do both simultaneously. The last thing I want to do is advocate some form of church planting and community transformation where groups take sides and yell at each other in blogs because they do not do things the way the other side does. Those on the community transformation side would pester church planters by making claims that they are simply about the worship gathering and not the community. Church planters would then fire off blogs in response to the community transformation people by saying they are too focused on doing good works and not proclaiming the Gospel and teaching people to worship God. These are needless debates that polarize groups. This does not create an environment for people to work together. Community transformation and church planting go hand in hand! They are two sides of the same coin and without one there is an imbalance.

The genesis of the tension for me was the realization that we can indeed plant a lot of churches but still have little to no impact on the surrounding community. For too long we were preoccupied with what took place on our church campuses and in our buildings. This is not a big church versus little church debate but more of an issue of the "tail wagging the dog." Many church planters start off with great aspirations to serve the community and play an active role in it. However, once the church is started, it can become consuming and much energy can be diverted to the gathering and discipling of people. Serving the community then becomes a backburner issue.

One of the key ingredients for church planters to engage in community transformation endeavors is to understand who they are as well as their community. For church planters to have an understanding of who they are, how God wired them, their gifts, passions, and abilities is pivotal. Community transformation flows out of who they are because it will have direct bearing of the direction in which they lead their new church.

When it comes to serving the community where does one even begin? It starts with the church planter and then moves to an understanding of their community. I mentioned the church planter first simply because of the reality that we are all wired and equipped to serve God uniquely. No two church planters are alike which means no two missional endeavors will be the same. The reason this is important because of our narrow view of how we can engage our community with the love of God in practical and tangible ways. For years I did not understand how to do this other than my own default thinking which was focused on feeding the homeless. If someone mentioned community transformation, all I knew of it was feeding the homeless, free car washes, or bringing cookies to elementary school teachers. I was basing community transformation on what everyone else was doing or what I read or heard about it. There was not much creativity.

One of the biggest differences between church planting the first time versus this second time around for me is that I understand better who I am and how God made me. The first time I planted I did everything that the books, training, and conferences told me to do. I was a greenhorn so how did I know anything different? So, I went with what all of the specialists said to do. My own ideas of church planting were just beginning to form and it was a completely new concept for me. It is natural to piggyback on others at this point.

Years later I am doing things completely different. I finally realized that I am similar to the quarterback Brett Favre more than anyone else. I do not mean in regards to success or anything like that but, in the great disparity of what makes him good and lousy at the same time. Of course, immediately mentioning him dates the book because who knows if he will retire, when he will retire and if he does he will simply come back with another team. I think even when he is seventy-six years old there is a chance he will still come out of retirement and play. I fully expect him to probably unretire in his 50s and play for 10 more years up here in Canada in the CFL. Brett is Brett and is a polarizing player with an equally polarizing personality. He will make brilliant plays that leave you in wonder and awe. Some of his throws seem humanly impossible as he zips the ball in triple coverage for a perfect touchdown throw. On the other hand, his assets quickly turn into liabilities. Those same amazing plays can instantly turn into abysmal failures where he loses playoff games because of late game interceptions. Brett is Brett. His greatest strengths are also his greatest weaknesses. With Favre though you know exactly what you're getting.

Church planters are like that. We all are. Our great assets can also be our greatest liabilities. I think one of the reasons why, despite all of his retiring, unretiring, and switching teams, people love him is that he is raw and seems like the real deal. If one is a Brett Favre fan he will take you to great heights and moments later to the depths of agony. The relevance in church planting is that all church planters bring great strengths and assets to the endeavor. Be confident in how God has wired and created you! Do not try to be anyone else! Favre cannot be like any of the other quarterbacks. It simply would not work and vice versa. When it comes to community transformation, church planters have every right to be themselves, knowing that the same Holy Spirit is indwelling them and all other believers. As a result they will be who they are and engage the community likewise. Do not worry about copying or mimicking what other churches or church plants are doing. That is unique to them, their city, their setting, and to the leader. What new forms of community transformation are out there to be explored?

As important as it is for the church planter to know themselves, it is essential for them to understand their context. This couples together who they are with the immediate needs and uniqueness of their neighborhood, district, and community. Church planters or missionaries living in and loving their communities will see and feel the needs around them. They will also understand how they can be meeting these needs based upon who God created them to be.

Community transformation does not necessarily have to be a nebulous concept. More and more church planters are taking an interest in their community, a positive and encouraging trend. As this happens there will be continued exponential growth of creative ideas, non-profits, and ways in which new churches are serving and loving. We are on the crest of a great wave that is reorienting much of the way we do and be church.

# 7

# The Nature of the City

The shaping forces of cities play an enormous role in the geography of church planting. The decision of where to start a church in a metropolitan area is critical to the future trajectory of the church because the setting or context influences so much. The new church will forever be influenced whether it is urban or suburban, poor or affluent neighborhood, low density or high density, homogeneous or multi-cultural. Not only that, but whether it is gentrified urban, decayed inner city urban neighborhood, downtown core, new edge city suburb, inner ring old suburb, or anything in between. If church planters adopt a more organic view of the city, when one looks at the cultural soil that churches are placed in, like a plant, there are areas more conducive for certain types of churches than others. The city is the soil and it varies across the metro area.

When I worked as a hiking guide, one of the fun privileges was introducing people to the desert environment for the first time. Many outsiders have certain perceptions of the desert and even more misperceptions. What drove me to understand my environment was simply all of the questions I would field out on a typical hike ranging from desert flora and fauna, and topography, to the human history of the area. I spent countless hours reading books and researching online about the desert and more specifically the Sonoran Desert where we lived. To most, a desert is a desert, but after a while one realizes is there's an enormous distinction between the deserts found in the US. They range from the Sonoran to the Chihuahuan to the Mojave and then the Great Basin desert. There are numerous geographic and climatic differences that separate them from one another. One of the distinguishing points of each desert is the specific vegetation found in each. For example, the stately saguaro cactus is found in the Sonoran Desert which, has an area that comprises of a good portion of Arizona, a tiny sliver in California, and protrudes down into Mexico.

The saguaro cactus is found here and nowhere else in the other North American deserts. This realization ends up ruining many movies that are portrayed in the West. It is ironic and even humorous to see a train stop in an old western movie supposedly set in El Paso, Texas but it has the classic saguaro right next to the train platform. Not true. Why? The Sonoran Desert provides the perfect and unique conditions that make the growth of the saguaro possible. It is all about the right environment for these sentinels of the desert to germinate and grow. In a like manner, the city environments provide a whole smattering of different environments for churches to grow in that are unique to each setting.

While this notion is a broad sweeping generalization, it still note-worthy because it alludes to the cultural soil conditions at play in the city. Like the saguaro, certain parts of the city provide fertile soil for certain kinds of churches versus others. Notice I did not mention anything about how certain parts of the city are not fertile for church plants, because that is simply not true. It is simply that certain types of churches seem to do better in some parts of the city than others. If we pan the camera back we see these differences in the cultural soil in the regions of North America.

Recently I was in the Dallas-Fort Worth metroplex and was driving across the city with a friend from college who is on staff at a large church. As we sped down the freeway we passed mega-church after mega-church. I began asking about how many mega-churches he could estimate were in the metroplex. Mega-churches comprise of 2,000 or more people. His conservative arm-chair missiologist estimates were that there were at least 50 to 70 in that area alone. Why does Dallas-Fort Worth have so many but where I live in Vancouver, BC have maybe a handful in that classification? Cultural soil. Just like how the cultural soil is different from region to region, it is so in the context of a single city.

The forces shaping urban areas versus those in the suburbs are simply different in the same way that the one finds saguaro cacti in the Sonoran Desert and Joshua trees in the Mojave Desert in California. Earlier in the book I took time to briefly state some of the different forces facing our cities today. What makes it challenging is that what is shap-ing Vancouver comes out in different expressions in Chicago as well as London or Mumbai or Beijing. Part of the understanding is taking note of the distinction between urban and suburban. My goal is not to paint the picture of one in a better light than the other. They are simply differ-ent. Similarly, churches in each setting are different as well. This is where church planting intersects with the social sciences; one of the academic disciplines often misunderstood and overlooked by church planters.

I had a friend in a city in the western US recently email me asking if I could be listed as a reference for him on his resume. Knowing he was roughly two years into a church plant, I immediately asked him what was going on. Identifying and assessing potential church planters can sometimes be an arduous task. While assessors have many of the key qualities of a successful church planter clarified, it still is an art form rather than a science. I knew my friend scored well and, as a matter of fact, I believed he would be a stellar church planter. He was, indeed, doing a great job. What went wrong? Context. It is not that the context was wrong or anything like that but compared with other parts of the city, his context came with many more challenges. In this particular city, most of the fastest growing new churches, like in most cities, are in a suburban setting. My friend had planted in an urban environment which brings to the forefront a whole litany of social issues that may not necessarily affect the extremities of cities. There is an enormous difference between a very multi-ethnic section of the city going through outward migration in comparison to a predominantly Caucasian suburb that continues to have a steady stream of people moving in. If one out of three homes in an urban neighborhood are for sale because many are opting to move farther out of the city, it will have enormous social and economic implications. This phenomenon, coupled with a steady influx of minorities, will change the fabric of a community which, in turn, will have a direct bearing on a new church plant. Again, this is not to say that one part of the city is easier than another to plant a church in or one is superior over the other but to emphasize that they are indeed different. As a result, the types of churches in each setting, along with everything in between, must be unique to the social and cultural soil at hand.

Most often, church planters utilize demographic studies which include the average age of those in a designated area with other such factors as gender, ethnicity, socio-economic classification, and lifestyle grouping. Many will use these tools, and rightly so, but there is more going on in a city than this. The cultural soil dictates much of how churches are being planted, or at least it should. I firmly believe that cities ought to shape and influence the way we go about church planting. Too often church planters think they need to have the whole church identity and culture figured out long before they even move into their locale. That involves importing an outside model but one of the issues to consider is whether this import is foreign or indigenous. As much as I would love it I simply cannot import a saguaro cactus and grow it outside in Vancouver. The soil and climatic differences dictate where I can and cannot grow it. Too often church planters, who conceive of their church without the context of their city, run the risk of importing foreign models.

The longing for clear models is desirable. However, we mistakenly believe that the way churches done 2,500 miles away is good enough for our own city and we blindly import, failing to realize we just might be bringing in a non-indigenous expression of church. Obviously when it comes down to it church is church, but too often we fall in love with expressions of church that we've experienced in other places.

Sometimes those places are even in our same city but we fail to consider the cultural soil of our neighborhood. We are to continuously be exposed to and learn from churches around our city, country, and even throughout the world. This has an amazing cross-pollination effect and stimulates thinking. As globalization continues to pick up pace it is now common to be in church planting networks with planters from other continents. This already has had an impact on theology, as now there is a proliferation of conversations about a global theology. Historically, in the past number of centuries, most of theology was written by Caucasian theologians. Whether we like to admit it or not theology is always set in culture which shapes and influences the way in which we view Scripture. When Caucasian theologians were the theological voice for the global church, something was indeed missing.

Globalization has allowed room for theologians from all over the world to collaborate and even to see new ideas from developing countries rise to prominence. Theological reflection should not solely be from the voice of one ethnicity who comprise of only 13 percent of the global population. When Asians, Africans, Latin Americans, and others have a voice it creates a more holistic theological system because each cultural group brings forth scriptural insights that other groups may have missed. When global theology is done in collaboration it offers a sense of checks and balances, for example: the way many theologians in other parts of the world challenge the West's integration of the church with capitalism or consumerism. We can point out each other's blind spots. The same applies to learning from others in church planting. We can and should learn from the global church and at the same time plant churches that resonate with local culture. This is healthy and when this concept is neglected new churches slip into the trap of blindly importing ideas and models from elsewhere with no regard for their specific cultural and community needs.

Some cultural settings can make very gifted and talented church planters look brilliant and others can make equally gifted and talented church planters look like abysmal failures. This goes beyond mere techniques, but requires an admission that the cultural soil is different in each part of the city. Using an extreme example: we would have different expectations of a church planter in Dubai in the United Arab Emirates in comparison with suburban Atlanta. Why? We recognize the cultural and spiritual distinction. We have all known and/or heard of planters laboring with certain unreached people groups for years to see little or no fruit. Sometimes these pioneers return home feeling deflated and defeated. At the same time we have heard stories of churches exploding with exponential growth in other parts of the world. The obvious is that God knows no boundaries or borders and can choose in his sovereignty to stir up many cities and people groups, thus drawing them to himself. The other factor at hand is the spiritual soil and its fertility.

When one looks at the spiritual soil of the first century, one sees there were, indeed, fertile conditions for the church to germinate and explode with growth. Peter's first message was to God-fearing Jews in Jerusalem. They already followed and worshipped God, so they knew the Hebrew Scriptures well. Peter simply plugged Jesus into the equation and it clicked for thousands who embraced him as the Messiah. Their worldview was already grounded in the reality of God, but they were missing one significant component. Often times, we take Jesus into contexts where there is no root memory of Christianity or even monotheism. While the US is a mission field, it still has predominantly a Judeo-Christian worldview and like, the first century, what many simply need is for Jesus to be plugged in to the equation. But what about other cultures and countries that have no Judeo-Christian worldview to begin with? What if their shaping influences were such things as Hinduism, Islam, Buddhism, Marxism, or animism? There needs to be a different starting point here. I remember listening to Ray Bakke talk in one of his lectures about the spread of the Gospel during the time of the early church in the first century. With Paul's Europe-bound trajectory, Ray surmised that maybe the reason why God pushed the Gospel in that direction was cultural. To the east were strong cultures in India and China. These beautifully rich and historic cultures were vastly different than that of their European counterparts. The cultural soil at the time, with the aid of common Greek, cemented the rapid spread of the Gospel into Europe and North Africa. The Roman culture provided the right cultural conditions in the Mediterranean for the expansion of the Gospel and the growth of the church.

The same understanding of the city is crucial. There is little doubt to the cultural differences in the city and its effect on church planting and the growth of new churches. I have friends locally who are church planters among the Punjabi Sikhs in metro Vancouver. Out of roughly 150,000 there are possibly 60 known Christians. In two years they have been able to pull together a house church of ten to fifteen adults. That is a completely different setting than a predominantly Caucasian middle-class edge of the city suburb. When it comes to expectations there is little doubt that we would have different ones for each church planter. Again, this is not a right versus wrong kind of scenario but to point out that cultural differences are important to understand as they have enormous shaping influences in church planting. This also brings forth tension on the geography of church based upon the way church planting has been done the past few decades.

Many funding models for church planting often have a three to five year window with each successive year seeing possibly a 20 percent decline in monies. Most church planters I know, myself included, feel that tension and live with it daily. There is a subconscious and invisible clock ticking with the realization that there are only three to five years to get the church to be financially self-sustaining. If we are completely honest we must then ask the question of where is the best setting to plant a church that would be financially self-sustaining in that timeframe? I will take it a step farther and question out loud as to how much of a motivating factor this is for site selection for church planting. Do not misunderstand what I am trying to get at, but this is a real life issue and an important piece of the church planting process to consider. Most church planters have families to take care of and bills to pay. But if one is pressed on the topic there is little doubt that there would be a consensus as to what part of the city would favor one type of church planting over other parts. Is this the reason why new growth suburbs and trendy gentrified districts get far more church planters than those areas with more lower class families? My goal is to not set up church planters in one part of the city as superior or inferior with those in other parts nor is this a discussion of who is right or wrong. I wanted to make mention of these issues because they are important to sort through.

Immigration has been a massive shaping influence in the US and Canada. Unless we are Native Americans (or First Nations in Canada) then our roots and entry points are as immigrants. As each successive wave of immigrants finds their way into North America it reconfigures the urban environment, most notably in Canada. One cannot fully understand Canadian cities without understanding immigration. Even two cities of similar size in the same region are radically different because of immigration. Although Seattle and Vancouver, BC are only a couple of hours from one another, any traveler to both cities will immediately be struck by the cultural differences. Because of immigration Vancouver is one of the most culturally diverse cities in the world. As urbanization, globalization, and immigration continue picking up pace, they are altering the very fabric of cities. This will have a significant impact and influence on church planting for the future. My impression of much of church planting training is that it is geared towards Caucasians who are planting in Caucasian majority middle-class suburbs. There needs to be a new paradigm as the nations of the world continue to stream into our cities. In my neighborhood I can talk to immigrants from China, Croatia, Romania, India, and Iran in a 10 minute span and all while sitting in Starbucks. The nations are here and the people moving to our cities still retain ties to their homeland. Many came here for a better life, job opportunities, or simply escaping for their lives.

I have heard many heart-breaking stories that my sons relate to me from their friends in elementary school who fled to Canada because of the dangerous conditions in their country. This has impacted me in ways that I cannot describe. For a while there was a young teenage neighbor who would have friends over from time to time. I would see this group of thirteen-year-olds always sitting outside smoking cigarettes. At first I was put off by that and wondered what kind of parent would let their thirteen-year-old smoke two packs a day. Over time I began talking to them and attempting to build a relational bridge. One evening as I was out walking our dog in the neighborhood, one of the chain-smoking thirteen-year-olds approached me. He asked if he could borrow my cell phone so he could call and get a ride home from his parents, so I let him. As soon as he got on the phone he began speaking in some language I was not familiar with. After he was finished he politely handed it back to me and thanked me. I decided to sit and wait with him while his parents were on their way because it was getting late. Since I was curious, I asked him what language he was speaking and so he told me. I then proceeded to ask where he was from and he told me how he recently moved from a country in Eastern Europe. My first response was, "Cool! How did you like growing up there?" I will never forget what followed next.

He went on to explain that he and his family had fled to Canada to escape a violent city. All of his younger siblings, all of the way down to an 18 month old, were shot and killed simply because they had the wrong color of skin. He learned to carry a gun to protect himself. When I heard that I could not help but feel great sorrow and even guilt for my initial judgmental attitude towards this young teen. Now it all made sense. "Do you know what?" I told him. "I am so glad you are here in Canada. I really believe that God saved you and brought you here for a purpose." While he shrugged this notion off I felt in my heart that I had to tell him that he is still loved and cherished by God despite the insurmountable pain and difficulties. When the nations come to our cities it may not always be neat and tidy. Cultural differences are enormous. When walking in our neighborhood some people make eye contact and smiles are normative while other cultures will not look someone in the eye in passing. I am learning these things as I navigate my own neighborhood.

I knew I was called to the Pacific Northwest. What made Vancouver stand out was the diversity. It continues to baffle me on a daily basis who I run into, the conversations I hear but do not understand, and how the global village now feels small since we all live within a few blocks of one another. For the first time in my life I am both a minority in ethnicity and in nationality. One of the baristas whom we have befriended is from Iran. It has been fascinating learning about her background, growing up in Iran, and the circumstances as to why she moved to Canada. In explaining where I came from, we began talking about our own neighborhood here. I said that as a Caucasians American I am indeed now a minority migrant worker here in our community in metro Vancouver. We laughed. I was told that when it comes to the list of countries of origin where Vancouverites are from it is not until down in the 30s that the US is even found. The number one country of origin is China. All of this has an enormous impact on the process of church planting. Most often it is in urban areas where the densest forms of diversity are found. To say that one model fits all for starting new churches is absurd. We need new forms of churches that are being pioneered in urban areas that differ from their suburban counterparts. The dynamics of the city warrant such differences.

City dynamics are ever changing and complex. As cities grow so do their complexities. It is similar to family life. There are enormous structural and relational changes that take place in a family transitioning from one to two to three children and so on. It is more than simply adding a new family member. It reorients the family structure and relationships. The same with the cities as they expand, decay, revitalize, densify, and diversify. The wider the variety of cultures introduced in a particular setting the more complex the social interactions. This has far reaching ramifications for church planting. In city after city, it is common to find specific ethnic churches. We have Chinese churches, Hispanic churches, African American churches, African churches, Iranian churches, French-speaking churches, Korean churches, and on down the list. While this is quite normative, it tends to lower the complexity of church planting since there is a shared cultural identity, language, and familiarity. Some make the case that churches need to be targeted for specific ethnicities in a city while others make the case otherwise.

It is easy to lose sight of the fact that there is a large chasm between a multiethnic church versus a multicultural one. Some churches indeed are multiethnic but they still share a common culture like young urban hipsters in a specific geographic district downtown who all speak English. Where does one go in culture to find models of various cultures, ethnicities, and even socio-economic groupings sharing space together?

While I was working on my doctorate at Bakke Graduate University in Seattle we would sometimes go for walks around downtown as a class. Since a major component of the program was studying cities there was no better way to do so than to get out and walk the streets. Our classes were held in the downtown which made it easily accessible for walking tours. Ray Bakke would lead the class on these city tours. We were given ear-pieces that made us look like undercover government officials. Actually they were speakers so we could all listen to Ray talk about the city while he spoke into a lapel microphone. Like a herd of cattle we would follow him around the city and listen to him explain what we were seeing, the shaping forces of the city, its history, and a theological understanding of the city. When we arrived at the famous Pike Place Market, the school had us break up into teams and walk around the market. The objective was to answer a series of questions based upon our observations. In particular, what can the church learn from a place like Pike Place Market?

What can the church learn? How is this relevant for church planting in urban contexts? What can we learn from the city and pervasive culture around us? When one mills around Pike Place or any similar settings, there are numerous cultural nuances converging in one place. It is a beautiful cross section of the city . . . rich, homeless, middle class, singles, families, young, old, not to mention the amazing diversity of ethnicities. How do places like this do it? How can a simple market be a reflection of the city and yet often times churches tend to focus on a particular age group or ethnicity? How does my local Starbucks do the same? Presently, while I sit here, there are eastern Europeans, Chinese, and Persians all sipping coffee in one place? Is this simply not a fair question because it is reflective more of consumerism than cultural patterns? Can we even distinguish? If cultures blend and meld throughout a community, then why are our churches so often homogeneous? What does Starbucks or Pike Place Market have that we do not? My attempt here is not to make sweeping accusations of the church or belittle her. Instead, my objective is to point out that through observation, there is much to learn from the city. I have made the case numerous times on my personal blog, and believe it is worth reiterating: most often, our cities will tell us how to go about planting a church if we would only observe and listen.

This goes back to church planting models and our love for them. When we blindly import models or ways of doing or being church from elsewhere, we lose out on the thorough process of exegeting our city and seeing local expressions of church birthed from within. Instead of rushing to get to the worship gathering, what if church planters took ample time to really understand their city, its past, its place among other regional and global cities, migration and immigration patterns, its values, strengths, deficiencies, and trajectory? The city is more than simply a collection of concrete, glass, and steel. Its overarching culture and vibe leads us to believe it is more of an organism than a mechanism. It is more living than robotic. In some ways it is as though the city is alive and has not only a personality but a collective spirituality. When we understand more the nature of the city, it serves as an aid in starting new churches and seeing community transformation take place. We become students of the city.

More than a mere academic pursuit, it becomes a dance of courtship as we pray for the city, fall in love with it, and ask God to redeem it.

The view of the city in which the church planter holds onto reveals much. If the city is a sin-infested impersonal machine, then that will shape and influence the new church's involvement in it. For too long the church has held on to an anti-urban bias which has had a detrimental impact. I believe this is one of the factors which on a subterranean level, leads church planters to the suburbs. This becomes problematic indeed to clearly bring to light, because it lurks in the depths of one's being. If someone were to ask me why I did not plant my first church in the city, I would not have been able to clearly articulate my bias against the city, but it was there. Cities were to be feared, viewed with skepticism, and were bastions of corruption and negative influences. The suburbs were safer and, of course, the best place in my mind to raise a family. Are they really safer? I recently read of a study by a university professor who investigated tragic deaths in cities. He combined homicide with vehicular death together and the results were staggering. The reality is that you have a better chance of being killed in the suburbs than in urban areas! Sure, the study combined homicide and vehicular death, but death is death, whether it is through a head-on collision or a gun shot. In an ironic twist, the suburbs were deemed more dangerous than the city. So much for raising a family in the safety of the suburbs! The point is not to criticize the suburbs, but to create tension so that we at least question our underlying biases and assumptions. I have always heard that the safest place to live is in the center of God's will but for many that is indeed a dangerous place. We have combined safety with middle-class values and with North American evangelicalism which leads us to living sanitized lives. Much of this stems from our understanding of the city and how we view it.

Cities are more than endless roads and freeways, houses, glass and steel towers, businesses, and people. Jesus wept over some cities and condemned others. In Luke 10:13 we find Jesus referring to various cities. "Woe to you, Chorazin! Woe to you, Bethsaida! For if the mighty works done in you had been done in Tyre and Sidon, they would have repented long ago, sitting in sackcloth and ashes." The question is who or what is he condemning? Is he talking about condemning the streets, bricks, walls, ports, businesses, or homes? No, Jesus is condemning the people. But not every individual was corrupt in Chorazin were they? Collectively, as a city, they emitted an overarching spirituality that was evil and ungodly.

The city was more than its built environment and more akin to a living and breathing spiritual entity. Not only did Jesus harshly rebuke cities, but also, he wept over them. "As he approached Jerusalem and saw the city, he wept over it."[1]

When it comes to understanding cities for church planting, there is much to consider. I have briefly mentioned such components as diversity and the collective personality and spirituality of a city, but there is another piece of the puzzle worth mentioning. Our view of the city needs to continue to expand. It goes beyond simple demographic studies as well. To understand the dynamic forces that shape cities, one needs to also take into consideration issues like transportation and the built environment as viable influential forces. In looking at transportation, a pertinent question to figure out is: how people get around in the city? That shapes the overall culture and even how church is to be done. I saw this stark contrast recently on a trip to Dallas. The sprawling city dumbfounded me and the endless freeways were baffling. I am used to living in a compact city center where everything is walkable. The first night I got to my hotel in one of the suburbs I was immediately struck by how far it was separated from every other business and everything else. It would be impossible to be car free in the sprawling suburbs. Everything revolved around the use of the auto, which has a direct bearing on church planting. It can be challenging to have an immediate impact on a local neighborhood if the church is not even rooted in one to begin with since it sits just off the freeway amidst other businesses. Transportation has a shaping influence on cities as well as church planting. Will the new church be a commuter church or rooted in a community? In contrast, other cities, or different parts of the same city, are denser whereby many residents get around on public transportation, bike, or foot. If a neighborhood is walkable with all necessary amenities within a few block radius of where one lives, it has a profound impact on church planting.

One of the reasons why we have chosen to plant Ion Communities in the various city centers across metro Vancouver is because of the ease of access and walkability that they provide. One of the ideas behind the city centers is to create dense mixed-use developments where one can live, shop, and play all in the same neighborhood. This is a pivotal concept that directly shapes church planting. I began thinking about ease

1. Luke 19:41.

of access to the church as a people. What if church life revolved around being pedestrian-friendly? What if it was the antithesis of the commuter church? Invariably, the proliferation of the mega-church movement came on the heels of the rise of the automobile. Would we have mega-churches if people simply worshipped where they lived? This is not to criticize the mega-church, but an attempt to point out the influence of transportation in a city and its density. For us, our focus is on each city center and those who live there. It is to make church body life accessible via foot, bike, or transit. Besides, is not part of living in community having a communal nature to it? What is the 24/7 church like when most everyone lives within walking distance of one another? A consideration of the city's transportation infrastructure will aid church planters in figuring out the how of church planting.

Another pertinent issue in understanding the city that is influential in church planting is the built environment. This goes hand in hand with understanding transportation. Transportation is often a reflection of the built environment of the city. A church planter needs to ask basic questions like how the city is laid out. What does my city's built environment show or teach me? Is the way my city was built offering me any insights into the best way to start a church in the area I am looking at? Some cities are dense and compact while others are spread out and sprawling and yet others have a good mix of both. This has a direct bearing on how church planting should take place. The idea behind this is to identify the forces that shape cities. Every city is unique and even each part of the city is different than the next. I assert that church planting should be a highly contextualized process. When church planters have already determined how they are going to do and be church even before they move to their new city they have failed to consider the city. That is not to say they will be failures by any stretch. Walmart or Starbucks can be uniformly found across North America as successful ventures. The question is a matter of importing church from elsewhere or starting churches that are reflective of the host city. The city is a great teacher if we would only pause and listen.

The layout of the city is an interesting element to look at. Cities are complex and baffling to understand. One can spend one's entire life studying a city and still not fully understand all of the dynamics at work and those who live within. On top of that, there are vast cultural differences in one part of the city compared to the next. Today I rode the Skytrain and bus for an hour to one of the suburbs on metro Vancouver's periphery. As soon as I stepped off the bus, I immediately noticed and felt the differences both in the built environment and the culture. This is a classic low-density sprawling suburb that is much more homogeneous than the city the further one gets out. From my vantage point at the Starbucks I could only see Caucasians, whether patrons or baristas. These two factors alone, if those were all of issues at play; have enormous shaping influences on church planting here versus other parts of the city. I am not advocating one part of the city is better than the other in the same way I would not deem one music genre better than another. The reality is that I have preferences in both but also know well enough that what is good and acceptable in my mind is not necessarily normative for others. This factors in how God made us, our background and upbringing, and so much more.

Urban versus suburban church planting debates in regards to what is better are simply an unhealthy conversation to have. Both are good and both are needed. The point in all of this, and even the scope of this book, is to bring to light the differences in culture, built environment, and transportation which must dictate how church planting is to be done. Where many get in trouble is to apply church planting templates or models that are not good fits for where they are planting. The difficulty is that in much church planting training systems, seminars, conferences, workshops, and books there is no distinction made for the various parts of the city. We blindly assume that since a church may be successful because of numeric growth, it becomes a worthy model to export widely. I believe we have yet to see all of the amazing ways that God will grow his church if planters will simply let go of models from their superheroes and focus on being the church in their setting thus allowing God to do a new thing. One of our values for the Ion Community is to plant walkable churches. Now I understand that some may bike, take transit, or even drive but the idea behind it is to create places of worship that are accessible by all and align with the city center concept of the city. This works for where I live and for other dense parts of the city, but it would be unpractical to make this an absolute in all parts of the city as well as other cities. Out here in Langley's city center, where I am today, anchored by a shopping mall, strip malls, and an endless ocean of concrete, it would not be practical or doable to have a walkable church. This is but one of many examples of the cultural and built environmental differences between the suburbs and the city. The goal is to plant churches that relate to and take into consideration these differences and so many more. The apply-all template cannot work and there needs to at least be a conversation in the prep work for church planting about this.

One of the great tragedies that came up from the surveys for the research for this book was the numerous churches that lacked engagement with the city. I saw this in my first version of the survey. This also has implications in the suburban and urban church planting conversation. Many blindly assume that simply having a worship service is enough. Although the idea is not new, do those who live around churches even know or feel their presence beyond seeing the buildings? In my city, I see many religious buildings from mosques to Sikh temples, to Buddhist temples and churches. To the uninitiated, what separates these from one another? Is there a difference? Do the religious activities that take place within each building have a direct impact or influence in the surrounding community? If we as the church are no different, then what is the problem? Do many people simply drive by daily and see there is a church and assume that inside spiritual activity takes place? Is that what we have relegated ourselves to? Doing spiritual activity in a building possibly a few times a week and that is it? Is that how we have defined what it means to be a follower of Jesus? We sing songs, listen to a lecture, and then go home. Is that what Jesus called us to? Did Christ die for that? What are we missing? The tragedy is that if we are good enough we can get a lot of people to do this all at once and we are deemed a success and yet the surrounding community sees little to no impact. What if the church came up with different criteria by which to measure itself? Instead of attendance numbers what if it was about involvement in the community?

This becomes a conversation that is deeply rooted in the context of the city. Community transformation must look different in neighborhood after neighborhood and city after city and suburb after suburb. One of the flaws in our thinking is in the areas of social engagement in our communities. What does community transformation even look like in a dense city core versus a sprawling middle class suburb? The needs in both places are real and yet different at the same time. Too often, when Christians think of serving their city the default mode is to feed to homeless, which is indeed important. I know of numerous churches that will drive youth from the suburbs to the downtown eastside of Vancouver to hand out sandwiches to the homeless. For many this is incredibly eye-opening and we know from Scripture that this is close to God's heart.

What about serving people in their community as well? What does that even look like when most everyone is in the same socio-economic grouping, live in single family detached homes, own two cars, and so on? There might be an occasional homeless person making their way through but it is not normative. What are the immediate needs? How can new churches meet those needs? How does one even find out? One of the difficulties is that often these needs are not blatantly clear but they are still present. The question we continuously ask ourselves is what are the needs in our community? How do we connect with people and meet tangible needs? Part of it is understanding one's community and the other part is seeing who God has crafted the church planter and the new church plant to be. Not every church planter or every church is equipped to meet all the needs but can do a few things well. Focus on those in light of the surrounding community.

The shaping forces in the city have a profound impact on church planting. So far in the book, several of these have been brought to light from gentrification to urbanization to globalization to immigration to transportation to the city's built environment to diversity, just to name a few. Each of these influences the city in major ways as well as church planting from within. Since cities are dynamic, they are ever changing whether in the life cycle of various neighborhoods, densification, or outward development. It is like hitting a moving target. Church planters would do well to have a deeper understanding of the social sciences and urban planning and to see the city with a different set of lenses. One of the shaping forces leading into the next chapter is that of the reorientation of North America's economy. This shift to a knowledge-based or creative economy has enormous implications for the future for our cities and church planting as well. The question is how well new churches are engaging this group with the Gospel both in word and deed.

# 8

# Church Planting and the Creative Class

The Creative Class has been an elusive and captivating group of people for me to seek to understand. I was first exposed to the idea while living in Tucson and tracking the beginnings of the downtown revitalization. I do not recall exactly how I heard of the term but it led me online to learn more and eventually to the writings of Richard Florida. I was a sponge and sought to read as much as I could as quickly as I could. It was as though scales began falling from my eyes as I began to understand the city more thoroughly and some of the influencing factors and forces shaping them. I have been on this journey now for a number of years and am only at the beginning of my own understanding. This learning and exploration was part of the genesis of my writing as well.

Of keen interest to me personally, as well as for this book, is to take a deeper look at gentrified neighborhoods and church planting in those locales among the Creative Class. It is a fascinating experience seeing and learning about various neighborhoods in cities across North America go through this gentrification process. Cities are like the ocean tide, constantly moving people in and out of the city like shells being picked up or deposited along the shoreline. City centers were once vibrant places to live, and when many of them, not all, fell on hard times, people left to go out farther to the safer and newer suburbs. Over time, these same urban communities were transformed and people started coming back into the city, often fueled by the presence of the Creative Class.

In my survey sent out to all church planters, I added a second section that was applicable for those who were planting a church in gentrified neighborhoods in and among the Creative Class. I clarified both what I meant by gentrified neighborhoods as well as the Creative class. For summary, gentrification can be defined broadly as the restoration and upgrading of deteriorating urban neighborhoods by affluent and middle income peoples, resulting in displacement of lower-income people. I was curious to see what it was like to plant churches in these types of communities where, while it can be trendy to live, there is also great social tension between the have-nots who live there and the haves who are moving in. Are these new church plants involved in these kinds of social issues, or do they tend to lean to one side of the social strata or the other? In my survey I sought to ask these church planters how they were going about church planting in gentrified neighborhoods, as well as if they were interacting with the Creative Class. Here are the questions asked to the church plant-ers in the second section of the survey:

1. Are you in a gentrified neighborhood or district? (If so, what is its name?)

2. Most often those who are part of what economist Richard Florida has dubbed the Creative Class are found within gentrified neighborhoods.

   A. How are you engaging the Creative Class in evangelism both in word and deed?

   B. How is planting a church in and among the Creative Class similar/dissimilar to what takes place in most church plants that you see around?

At this point, out of all the church planters who filled out the survey (which was 25 percent), roughly one-third of them identified themselves as being in gentrified neighborhoods. Since this was a very narrow and specific location choice, I knew the numbers would actually be low be-cause by sheer numbers, the bulk of church plants are in the suburbs. However, the responses and feedback were still valuable and pertinent. Out of the seven focus cities, I received responses from church plant-ers in five cities; Vancouver, Seattle, Portland, Albuquerque, and Denver. Missing were Phoenix and Tucson. I believe that part of the reason was the lack of church plants found in the downtown core of cities or in neigh-borhoods going through gentrification. Tucson had no church plants in the downtown core that I was aware of at the time of the research, and 85 percent of church plants found in Phoenix were suburban. Another pos-sible reason Tucson had no responses is that gentrification is not as wide spread as found in other cities. In contrast, cities like Vancouver, gentri-fication is so widespread, it is difficult even to keep up whether urban or suburban. Even where I am today is a suburb, but the neighborhood is going through extensive gentrification with new high-rise condos across the road from low income low-rise apartments. There have been massive changes over the past five years and the next five will reveal even more.

## ENGAGING THE CREATIVE CLASS

My first question was simply to ask if these church planters were in a gentrified neighborhood and then to give the name of that community. Most of the church planters who responded to the survey gave me the name of their neighborhood. In some cases there were several church planters in the same neighborhood. On the other hand, there were some church planters who may have been working with the Creative Class but were not located in a gentrified neighborhood. Once they identified themselves as being in a gentrified neighborhood, I went on to ask them how they are engaging the Creative Class with the Gospel both in word and deed. I will list below some of the responses and then make some observations following.

1. We are trying to engage in life and worship fully—emphasizing the creativity of God—and that our creativity is both gift to each other and a means of restoration for us. People who engage with us recognize how we value creativity and embrace the creative. We regularly have meetings and focus on freedom and creativity and worship.

2. We make the arts and story telling a big part of our smaller and larger gatherings.

3. I am part of a team of people (False Creek Residents Association) who are working with city planners regarding the development of North East False Creek. In doing this, I have made presentations at City Council and rubbed shoulders with my neighbors, urban planners, and city councilors.

4. Through their natural networks.

5. Prayer, technology, internet, personal relationships, and service to their children.

6. We largely interact with them by supporting their families (especially their kids) and provide opportunities for parents and

kids to interact.

7. The Alpha Course and community festivals.

8. We have many "representatives" from The Open House engaged in everyday life with this class as many of our group is in this class.

9. In word via conversations as neighbors, by deed by reaching out to folks to contribute to non-profits and initiatives that are already underway.

10. Music and the arts through open mic's, B-Boy and Rap Battles, concerts, plays, writing/dancing workshops, recording options, etc.

11. Social justice, blessing the school and neighborhood.

12. One, through aesthetics on our website and in our space. Two, through an organic, decentralized structure allowing the vision and ethos of the Gospel changing culture and bringing justice to the community. We will do much more interactive worship, hands on community service, and freedom to be spiritual in all areas of life.

13. We are working to build a culture that increasingly draws creative people and unleashes that creativity in its most powerful ways—by the Spirit.

14. Hosting various discussion groups in neighborhood pubs, coffee shops, etc. Our people are actively involved both as a collective body and as individuals in all sorts of things in the neighborhood—music festivals, arts festivals, supporting local businesses. It's taken a while, but presence has really been the biggest deal for us. Being seen and known in the neighborhood has been huge.

15. Emphasis on worship arts, offering performing arts space and social justice.

16. Praying for God to give us boldness, then engaging through invitation to sit in Scripture.

17. Intentional balance of "spiritually vibrant" and "intellectually honest" in our ministry approach. Empowering congregants to

minister in their sphere of influence or area of interest. Creating a variety of relationship opportunities upstream of service opportunities. Presenting the church as a sort of ministry co-op—a kingdom mutual fund—comprised of investment-savvy members.

After compiling and reading through the surveys, I was left with more questions than answers. Of all areas of my research, this area has been by far the most frustrating and difficult to put parameters around, whether I am talking about gentrified neighborhoods or planting churches among the Creative Class. While I may have an understanding in my mind what both of them are or what they look like, I have learned that everyone seems to have a different view on it. Sometimes gentrification is easy to spot and put a finger on, and at other times it may not be reflective in numerous new coffee shops and pubs or new construction or redevelopments because it is simply early on in the process. I am also relying on the church planters surveyed in this section as well as their understanding of gentrification and the Creative Class, and I did attempt to define them both. It seemed like some of the church planters had an acute awareness of gentrification and the Creative Class. They knew exactly what I was talking about and had a clear understanding themselves and even had read some of Florida's books. On the other hand, I had some church planters fill this out who were in far flung suburbs where in some settings I knew gentrification was not taking place. What is difficult to also place is the geography of where the Creative Class lives. Not all of them live in the city in trendy lofts furnished with Ikea furniture above a coffee shop in a gentrified neighborhood where they can ride their moped to the organic grocery store or gather vegetables in their co-op garden. Creative types also live in the suburbs, have families, drive mini-vans, vote conservative, and do not recycle.

Along with the tension of clearly identifying gentrified neighborhoods is the reality of fully describing and realizing who the Creative Class is. Again, this term can be somewhat nebulous and difficult to fully explain. For example, for a few years now I have been reading all of Richard Florida's books, keeping current with his blogs, following him on Twitter, reading other reviews of his works, as well as similar books out there, and I am honest enough to admit that after all of this time and work, it is still taking me a while to get my mind around what it means to be part of the

Creative Class and what exactly they look like. Many assume because of the title, the Creative Class is simply made up of starving artists, budding musicians, aspiring actors or actresses, and unwashed bohemians with dreadlocks. While these categories may indeed make up a small part of the Creative Class, those categories are not a full range of who they are according to Florida. So then, how accurate is the data I received from these church planters?

With all of those qualifiers set in place, I will look at their responses and analyze them. If I could be assertive and sift through them, I believe the responses would fall somewhere into three different over-arching categories for how to engage the Creative Class in gentrified neighborhoods.

1. authentic relationships

2. presence

3. creativity

The first popular category of reaching and connecting with the Creative Class would be that of authentic relationships. Like in any ministry contexts, relationships are vital and important, which also applies to the Creative Class. This reality might be even more pertinent and relevant in urban settings where there is such thick and beautiful diversity. Part of forming authentic relationships is simply being a friend. With the tech-driven frenetic pace of life that many who are part of this class live, slowing down to connect with someone face to face is invaluable. One church in Denver that was surveyed hosts various discussion groups in their neighborhood in pubs and coffee shops. These settings are the natural Third Places found in society and great intersecting places for people to connect. Numerous other church plants wrote about connecting with and supporting people in the Creative Class even down to their children where applicable. A church in Vancouver points out that since their church is made up of creative types this relational interconnectivity is encouraged and happens organically along the lines of natural networks of relationships.

Another dominant theme among those surveyed was the power of presence, which means that within new church plants in gentrified neighborhoods among the Creative Class, one of the best assets they have to offer is simply being there. While at first this may seem overly simplified and trite, there is something powerful and even culture shaping and changing about it. This response goes beyond merely having an address in the community, but instead, they see themselves as part of it, and in many ways, both in word and deed, they are weaving their church plants into the fabric of their neighborhoods. One church in downtown Vancouver is rubbing shoulders with urban planners and city leaders while another in Vancouver puts on community festivals for the people who live in a university community. An Albuquerque church offers performing arts space for the residents in the Nob Hill neighborhood where the church is now a mainstay. It seems as though many of these church planters have a well developed (or developing) theology of place, which acts as a rudder, guiding their church plants to be actively involved in their neighborhoods.

As far as the last main category, it would be appropriate to include creativity as a way that church plants in gentrified neighborhoods are connecting with the Creative Class. Determining how successful they are was not measured, but what I do know is that many are attempting to use creativity in the church planting process as well as in the body life of the church. Since creative types use their creativity and intellect as their means of income and occupation, it makes sense to utilize this factor in the church planting process. One of the church plants made mention of the creativity of God and how that is a gift to one another and a means to restoration. This idea seems to be pivotal in utilizing creativity; otherwise it simply becomes a utilitarian exercise.

Creativity for wider market appeal seems to stand in contrast to one of the other ways church planters are reaching out to creative types, which is through authentic relationships. Whereas presence seems to be rooted in a theology of place, creativity can be best rooted in the creativity of the Creator. A church in Vancouver explained how they make the arts and story telling a big part of their gatherings, including graphic design on their web page, a portable art gallery on Sunday mornings, creative songwriting to be expressed during their gatherings, poetry readings, etc. In a sensory-overloaded society, it makes sense for church plants to have creativity as one of the primary means to engage the creative class.

## THE UNIQUENESS OF PLANTING AMONG THE CREATIVE CLASS

The last question I asked in the survey is how church planting in and among the Creative Class was similar or dissimilar from what takes place in most church plants that particular church planters see around them in their city? From their vantage point I was curious to find out how they thought of church planting in their contexts as similar or different than what others are doing. Does church planting among the Creative Class truly differ? If so, then how? Here is how some of the church planters responded:

1. We foster an atmosphere of freedom of expression—which means we make room for it (physically, time-wise).

2. It is similar in that all mission work requires studying the prevailing culture and looking for Gospel markers within. In creative class communities—you simply must engage their creativity and weave the Author of all Creativity into the story. All cultures have idols—bohemians are no different. And these can be addressed through story, narrative & expository preaching in all cultures.

3. I am certainly not the only one attempting to do such things. We are all stumbling forward trying to figure out how to bring the Kingdom of God to the most post-modern city in Canada. We have to be willing to do things different than we did in the past. We have to be willing to be "the hands and feet of Jesus." This means we have to go into some very dark places: the world of high risk sex offenders, single room occupancy hotels (SROs), poetry slams where people talk openly of their gay or heterosexual lifestyle, addictions, counseling, etc.

4. Functionality—it is not that different—smart, creative, rich, high octane people still have dead souls—speak truth clearly.

5. To reach these people we need a wave of missionaries that will commit to do life and be the church in their everyday world. It will take a much longer period of time to reach them with the gospel and will require a more decentralized approach to ministry (engaging the 3rd spaces).

6. I do not see major differences.

7. Our aim is not to get people "in" the church, but instead to engage them where we live, work and play. I find that most churches are trying to get people to assimilate in the church at whatever time they meet.

8. I simply see it as higher octane in that the stakes appear to be higher by sitting at the table with big businesses, major political forces, and a high degree of interest in the neighborhood by the surrounding city. I also think that relocation and affordability are major issues, along with family housing (though less so in Vancouver than the States). Finally, I wouldn't have data on this, but my hunch is that the Creative Class tends to be farther down the post-Christendom line then more established urban neighborhoods, and especially most suburbs, which demands both more creativity and patience on the journey towards conversion, if conversion happens. Essentially, the normal "church planting rules" do not work here, at least not that I have seen work.

9. The specific challenge in our own church is to develop in our people an authentic compassion for people who are not necessarily like themselves as "like draws like" is as true in this church plant setting as it may be anywhere else.

10. Everyone is broken and in need of Jesus and the gospel, thus in that sense there is no difference between the homeless and those living in Mercer Island, but there is great difference in the needs, and reasons for brokenness, and traditional means to reaching creatives are often irrelevant, so I believe you need to engage their creativeness, and show both God's stamp on their creation as "Co-Creators" with Him, and their sense of loss and lack of Beauty because of sin and brokenness. The gospel is God's story that transcends culture and generations, and His story intersects with our stories redemptively; it's our task to display where that redemption is needed and who is it that ultimately provides it.

11. Many of the nationally recognized church planting strategies are not useful here as our neighbors are generally gospel resistant. The work here is not similar to how one might approach ministry in the suburbs or in a more conservative area.

12. Social justice needs to be a major emphasis.

13. Making sure they are involved in ownership of the process and are not being talked "to" or ministered "to." Also, very heavily involved in social justice issues of hunger, oppression, etc.

14. It is similar because of homogeny. People like people who like what they like / think how they think. Parenthetically, we find that it is not about race, gender, etc for us. Rather, it is about interests. I think the bottom line is that reaching creative people places creative leadership at a premium—and creativity never takes a holiday.

15. A lot of typical suburban church plants take a largely marketing driven approach. They spend $50,000 on fliers and some creative hook and try to get a critical mass that way. I am pretty sure our neighborhood would set fire to any mailers we would be tempted to send out. The creative class is extremely relational. They do not want to be sold something—especially the gospel or a particular church. So while a big show, lasers, and mailers may work in some contexts, I haven't seen it work among the Creative Class. We have a longer road, gathering is slower, gaining trust is slower, but I think the fruit is deeper and richer in the long run. All that being said, we are only 16 months in and we have a long way to go.

16. Far less program driven.

17. The Gospel is not hip or artsy. It's offensive. The Lord convicted me of my attempts to be contextually relevant. . . not that communicating clearly within the culture was of no value, but because it was usually some sort of apology for how much Jesus was going to demand of them. The Gospel was stripped of its power because I was not actually sharing the Gospel. I was, in my anthropological kindness, ushering people towards hell. My flesh is offended by the Gospel, and it's going to offend the Creative Class as much as it offended the 1st century audience that killed Jesus.

18. The demographic is less homogenous than outside the beltways of metro areas. Church is able to be less facility-centric. Constiutuents are less inclined to come to church asking, "What should I do?"

What I found through perusing through these and other responses was that it broke down into several different themes. While there could be more, I wanted to condense the answers into four wide-reaching general categories that most of the responses fit into.

1. There is no difference between planting in gentrified neighborhoods among the Creative Class compared to elsewhere.

2. There is and needs to be an emphasis on creativity in church planting among the Creative Class.

3. Social justice must play a primary role in these kinds of church plants in gentrified neighborhoods.

4. Diversity is valued given the nature of the city, gentrified neighborhoods, and even the preferences of the Creative Class.

A few responded by pointing out that there were no real major differences between planting in gentrified neighborhoods among the Creative Class than in other locations. On the surface level that seems to be a completely valid response and applicable to all. In reality being the church is being the church regardless of how one gathers, what they look like, what language is spoken, where Christians are gathered, what kind of music is sung, how Scripture is taught, and so on. The church was not a human invention and there are universal signs of what church is that transcends time and culture. Issues like language, music style, teaching techniques, and so on, play a secondary role to the bigger reality that the church is God's people gathering together to be the church. With that in mind then, church really does not differ from an urban gentrified neighborhood among the Creative Class compared to other parts of the city. The differences may be more cosmetic rather than truly foundational.

On the other hand, if one looks at it in a different light, there are differences based upon the cultural milieu that new churches are being planted in. Since churches are always contextual, then churches in gentrified neighborhoods ought to look different from the suburbs in the same way a rural church ought to look different from urban or suburban. One of the elements that may set apart planting churches in urban gentrified neighborhoods among the Creative Class is the value and need for creativity. Again, as Richard Florida points out, the Creative Class are those who draw their income, livelihood, or identity in using their creativity and intellect. Therefore, it does make complete sense to have this as part of the make-up of the church.

Creativity is also a theme in the way church planters go about engaging their community with the gospel. Set in a trendy neighborhood in Portland, one of the churches surveyed is immersed in the culture of bohemians, artists, and skeptics who make up the Creative Class. Their context demands a different approach, and in the survey, the insight from their church planter was key when he said, "Many of the nationally recognized church planting strategies are not useful here as our neighbors are generally gospel resistant. The work here is not similar to how one might approach ministry in the suburbs or in a more conservative area." Creative types do not seem to be as open to marketing techniques often used by churches in suburban settings. One church planter said, "A lot of typical suburban church plants take a largely marketing driven approach. They spend $50,000 on fliers and some creative hook and try to get a critical mass that way. I am pretty sure our neighborhood would set fire to any mailers we would be tempted to send out. The creative class is extremely relational. They do not want to be sold something- especially the gospel or a particular church. So while a big show, lasers, and mailers may work in some contexts, I have not seen it work among the creative class. We have a longer road, gathering is slower, gaining trust is slower, but I think the fruit is deeper and richer in the long run."

A major theme among the surveyed church planters in gentrified neighborhoods is that social justice is to be a primary focus. While the Creative Class does occupy a certain percentage of urban dwellers in gentrified neighborhood, they are not the sole residents. There are still often low income families living there and thus a heightened social tension between the haves and have-nots living on the same block. Church planters moving into these neighborhoods do indeed send a message. "When we move into a poor neighborhood, we send the message that if love is costly, then those who are the object of such love are worth much. This element is especially important to the poor who bear the weight of the world's low opinion of them."[1] When asked the question of whether their urban church plant is in a gentrified neighborhood, one church planter said that his area is the result of gentrification taking place further in towards the city center. They are dealing with the adverse effect of displaced and disenfranchised urban dwellers who were priced right out of their homes. It almost goes without saying that it would be difficult to live in and plant a

1. Hayes, *Sub-Merge*, 117.

church in an urban setting without being acutely aware of the needs of the community. Social justice seems to be a natural outflow for many of these churches who are seeking to integrate the gospel into their setting.

Lastly, there is a recognition of the value and need for diversity. It can be argued that what draws many of the Creative Class into the city and into gentrified neighborhoods is the value placed on diversity and freedom of expression. Urban settings like this are hotbeds for that kind of a lifestyle. It truly is stimulating being in complex urban environments where rich and poor live on the same block, as well as through social dynamics like immigration. It seems like the whole world is now living above, below, and beside urban dwellers. One church planter in Seattle wrote of this tension, "The specific challenge in our own church is to develop in our people an authentic compassion for people who are not necessarily like themselves, as 'like draws like' is as true in this church-plant setting as it may be anywhere else." Another church planter in Denver mentioned how, "The demographic is less homogenous than outside the beltways of metro areas."

Church planting in gentrified neighborhoods can be very complex and difficult based upon numerous social factors at hand. Every beautiful façade has a darker story behind it, and for every creative urban hipster, there is a low income immigrant family eking out a living in the service industry. The church planters surveyed seem to be aware of the social and physical dynamics present that make them emphasize the gospel as not only being transformative for individuals but as well for social structures and neighborhoods. This awareness goes hand in hand with the idea of community transformation that most church plants are involved in, whether urban or suburban, where the primary ways are partnering with the city through volunteerism to meet tangible and physical needs. The combination of the Creative Class, gentrified neighborhoods, and even a wider look at global cities, brings up several foundational questions: How does one live in the city as a follower of Jesus? What does an urban spirituality look like or is there even such a thing? What does church planting and community transformation look like? How do all of the shaping forces impacting cities affect us? These questions and more open the discussion for what I call "metrospirituality." This key concept is the topic moving through the rest of the book.

# 9

## Metrospiritual

Even through the double-pane window of a 10th floor hotel room, the sounds of the city have a way of infiltrating through the walls and disturbing one's sleep. Now that I think about it, I do not recall that the city-sounds ever went away because it was the same noise as when I went to sleep. Walking over to the window I peered through the haze to the city below. I could see that Shanghai was already awake and alive and it was only 6:15 AM. The streets were packed with people and vehicles with the sounds of honking mopeds and cars rising above the construction commotion. Jackhammers pounded bricks and concrete as old buildings were torn down to make way for ultra-modern skyscrapers. The city was not only alive but exploding with growth. Everywhere I looked seemed to be one enormous construction project.

After a shower I grabbed my laptop and headed out of the hotel to travel on foot. I wove in and out of pedestrian traffic, dodging the swarm of bicyclists and mopeds that easily sneak up if attention is not given. Many of the shops were already open with the smells of cooking food wafting through the air. The first leg of the journey on foot was definitely raw, nothing glamorous, and felt like old Shanghai. Most of the buildings were old, somewhat dilapidated or being torn down. However, in the span of a city block everything abruptly changed. Little family-run food stands and dark narrow alleys gave way to sophisticated and chic shopping malls, trendy restaurants, and of course ... Starbucks. My goal was to grab a latte, get out the laptop, and do some blogging and reading.

I have to admit that Starbucks is a great place to people-watch. The big windows afforded me the opportunity to not only watch in-coming customers but to follow the flow of foot traffic on the sidewalk in front of me. The crowd both inside and out tended to be young adults in their 20s and dressed to the hilt. Clean cut, modern, urban, and sophisticated. As I

146

sat there sipping on my latte watching the great mass of humanity in front of me, I tried to imagine what life was like for these young urbanites. In the background and all around were high-rise residential buildings so I was led to believe that most lived there or took the bus or subway to this area to work. I also began asking questions like: Who are these people? Where did they come from? Are they native to this city? Did they come from other regions? Did they grow up rural and come to the city to get a good education? Were they part of the mass migration in China from rural to urban? Lastly, what do they even know of God? If they were to access the Gospel, how would they do it and where? Are there any churches meeting in this area? If one were to start a church here, how would they do it? Where would they start? What would the process be? How would one begin to contextualize the message of Jesus and the formation of the church that would make sense to these people?

When it comes to church planting these are some of the beginning questions we need to wrestle with and sort through if we want to ultimately influence cities. Context is everything! The way we go about church planting will be different whether in Shanghai, Tokyo, London, San Francisco, Tucson, Omaha, or wherever one is planting. To blindly import non-contextualized models and procedures is a sure-fire recipe for disaster. More than a church planting mindset, there is something more subterranean that needs to be embraced when it comes to faith in the city. I have run into so many people over the years who look like a fish out of water in the city. I should know since I used to be like that as well. However, something changed. This transformation was not simply external like donning the attire of urbanites in a particular region, but a significant metamorphosis. It is not unlike the physiological change that takes place in a salmon as it leaves the fresh running water hemmed in by the river banks for the wide open expanse of the ocean full of salt water. The change is enormous. The salmon learns to breathe in something that was earlier foreign to it. If one were to take most any other fresh water fish and drop them in a salt water fish tank, they would soon die. My personal journey was and is like learning to breathe in something that was previously foreign to me.

This change is more than simply having an address in a particular city but learning to breathe in the city, love the city, embrace the city, weep over the city, and long for, plan, and trust God to transform it. *Metrospiritual* is the term that comes to mind. While I have yet to see the term in print it seems like the most useful term I can use to describe an urban spirituality. Since the term "urban" encompasses much, there is widespread application for it. Having been in and out of cities in North America and abroad urban comes to look and feel like something completely different in each setting. Urban Memphis, Tennessee is completely different than urban Vancouver. There are issues that plague American cities that for various reasons did not make their way into Canadian cities. That aside, what is metrospiritual? What does it look like? What are the parameters of it? Where did the idea of it begin weaving itself into my own thinking?

Throughout the book I tried my best to combine academic rigor with my own story. If academic writing provides the bones or structure of a book, my hope is that the stories, flaws and all, will at least begin to put flesh on those bones. I also did my best to be transparent with my own life; the struggles, the wrestling, and the journey. For every fault set forth in the book, I know of at least 10 others I have surrounding each issue so in no way was my goal to attempt to communicate some neat and tidy progression in my own life. Recently, I told my wife about writing the story of the brown bear into the book as I was pondering on the topic of calling. I remarked, "Well, it'll soon be out there for everyone to read. Why did I move to Vancouver? Well, um, a brown bear told me?" It is not necessarily an answer one is always up front with. We tend to couch things in terms of a sophisticated spirituality. Not so. I have purposely written this book with several components in mind.

First, I wanted to base it on research and overall general observations I was seeing at the time. Second, was to attempt to provide adequate ways to personalize and put into application the ramifications of the research. Lastly, I wanted to speculate. If the research has led me to certain conclusions that differ from the norm, which means a new way forward is essential. That is where metrospiritual comes in. I would like to take time now to begin fleshing out what an urban-centric faith looks like in church planting.

One of the first glimpses of the metrospirituality concept taking root in my life was on the same trip to China that I referenced at the beginning of this chapter. To no one's surprise, it came at a Starbucks, but it was in Beijing this time. We had the fortunate opportunity to be there right before the 2008 Summer Olympics, so we were able to at least drive by the main venues and soak in the vibe. The whole city seemed to be like a giant beehive with tens of thousands of workers frantically finishing up projects before the world's spotlight shone down on the city. The energy in the air was almost tangible. I believe that what the Olympics did was highlight progress that China continues to make in becoming a global economic power and a progressive nation. Certainly the various cities we were in were amazing!

Now back to the Starbucks story. When we had free time several of us would slip on over to the Starbucks to use the free Wi-Fi and drink coffee. At times I had to do a double-take to make sure I knew where I was because it did not even seem like I had left the US! Here I was sitting in Starbucks, next to the Apple Store, and ordering a vanilla latte in English since I do not know an ounce of Mandarin or Cantonese. On top of that, I linked up with other computer users who were at the Starbucks to share music files. What that basically meant was we could listen to music on each other's computers while we were online together. As I began looking through the playlists of the various local young adults, I was amazed that we were all listening to the same music. With few exceptions our playlists had the many of the same artists. Then it hit me. The world has indeed changed.

Metrospirituality is a global urban framework for following God. For centuries our predominant lens in which we viewed Scripture was with a rural bias. Metrospirituality is the opposite. It is taking an urban lens to the reading, understanding, interpretation, and application of Scripture. When this change began in me, suddenly I saw things I had never noticed before. I have read the Bible countless times and I have an undergrad degree in Biblical Studies which means I have taken course after course on the books of the Bible as well as theology. All of a sudden everything began clicking for me. I saw the Bible anew and it was and is exciting! For many, the part of the Bible that gets the least amount of visitors is the prophets. Chalked full of imagery, odd tactics, and lots of doom and gloom, these obscure books tend to be rather depressing to read. However, once I began to understand God's heart and plan for cities, which started back in Genesis, then even the prophets came alive. Prophets like Isaiah, Jeremiah, Ezekiel, and Zechariah began to make more sense to me than ever before. A metrospiritual framework is needed to read, understand, interpret, and live out God's Word.

Being metrospiritual asks questions surrounding what faith looks like lived out in the global city. What does it look like and how does it differ from the way we have previously lived, breathed, and thought of cities let alone church planting or community transformation within? God is doing something in the world that has never occurred in human history before. If we believe that God is sovereign, then we must conclude he is the driving force behind urbanizing the world. This trajectory was set forth from the very beginning in Genesis and will reach its culmination in Revelation. It is worth mentioning again, but I tell people that if they do not like cities they may not enjoy heaven and the New Jerusalem. Jesus is preparing a place for us to live for all of eternity that makes Tokyo and New York look like sleepy burrows. My only request is that I would live in a chic loft atop a Starbucks and an REI. Heaven will be an amazing place and we will enjoy a city that has no temple because we will continuously live in God's presence. Everything is spiritual, which is the core essence of a metrospirituality.

Metrospirituality affects everything I do in terms of my involvement in the city. The scope is much larger than simply church planting. We can plant churches at length without much impact, influence, or presence in our neighborhoods. I even go as far as telling people when they ask what I do for a living that I am a community developer. The goal is the whole community being transformed with the church playing one component and our urthTREK plays another. UrthTREK is an idea the began germinating in my imagination while in Arizona. Like I shared before, I was a hiking and mountain biking guide in southern Arizona for a number of years while I was involved in church planting. During that time I took literally thousands of people out into the wilderness hiking and biking. For many it was their first experience in outdoor adventure and they had never been on a mountain bike before or hiked in the mountains. Hiking and biking became a great tool in order to connect with people relationally. Many had come to get away from all the stresses and pressures in life. Once outdoors, it was evident how therapeutic the experience truly was. When out on a trail for several hours with a group of people, one realizes that there are only a couple of things at hand . . . each other, our stories, and the wide open wilderness. Whether it was clambering up a rocky ridgeline, strolling over the mountain's foothills, exploring an ancient Hohokam village site, or barreling down singletrack on a bike, it was an experience unlike most have gone through. The interpersonal connections and conversations that took place were amazing. At times guides would find themselves a listening ear as people talked about real life issues ranging from drug abuse, divorce, or burnout. But something was missing.

Most of the people who had accessed our services would be considered societal elites; high-powered business professionals, actors and actresses, athletes, and the like. It was so refreshing to get to know these wonderful people as we strolled through the wilderness where we were away from the distractions and stresses of life. However, I kept thinking of all the people who did not have access to such amazing experiences. In my free time, I took numerous people on similar outings, exposing them to the great outdoors for the first time. Many simply did not have the resources or know-how to do this and were grateful for the experience. In light of the emotional and physical release that people feel outdoors, I began to think of all the people who normally do not get this opportunity. What about school children in disadvantaged neighborhoods? Or battered women who would benefit greatly from a refreshing hike for a few hours? A bipolar support group having an outing to gain a fresh perspective on life? Or recent international immigrants who can explore the wilderness around their new city with guides who care? This is where was urthTREK was born.

It has already begun evolving since placing it in the context of my community here in BC. We have also begun adding elements like environmental education, classes or workshops, and are in the process of putting together a longboarding club for elementary students. This is not a bait-and-switch kind of endeavor where we trick people into participating with us and then we hold them hostage and tell them the Gospel. The following idea is not new to many: we do not serve people in order to convert them (not that I like the term "convert") but we serve people because we have been redeemed and we demonstrate that love in word and deed. A metrospirituality is taking perspective into consideration the whole community and seeing no difference in spiritual and physical needs. Again, if we hold to the notion that everything is spiritual, then there will be no dichotomy in our thinking. Is that why many Christians struggle to understand the Old Testament? We have made clear demarcations between the spiritual and the physical and that was never to be the case. In reality everything is spiritual and our physicality plays out what we truly deem to be spiritual or not. If we hold some things as spiritual or not it will be evidenced in our approach to them. If urban issues are not, indeed, spiritual at their core, we may apply the wrong remedies or only look at surface issues

For a while I struggled with the television show *Extreme Makeover: Home Edition.* The stories in each episode were all incredibly touching and on cue I would have to fight back tears. But then I began to perceive flaws in the whole concept. Was all of this simply an extension of American consumerism where people only felt good when they had nice things like others? Was it an issue of rampant materialism? Of course in conversations like this it is easy to mention impoverished people from developing countries living in squatter settlements as a basis of comparison to the way we live in North America. The guilt ensues. We then puff out our spiritual chest to think we are somehow mysteriously cool and ultra spiritual because we have seen through the farce of *Extreme Makeover: Home Edition.* However, there is something deeper and even more beautiful taking place here that goes beyond building new homes with nice landscaping and stunning interior decorating that we all dream of. One of the foundational elements at hand is that of basic dignity. It is not about consumerism or materialism but restoring something that had been lost or broken. Dignity. Most of the stories we are exposed to during the show are of heartbreak, great tragedy, or adversity. What the makeover does is help restore people's dignity which at its core is a very spiritual issue. I would make the case that dignity, is on God's heart as well. One of the components we lost in the Garden of Eden when sin entered the picture was dignity. We became rather base people. Something done in the physical like remaking a home is really a spiritual exercise. That is part of metrospirituality.

Metrospirituality embraces the city. It sees that physical issues are spiritual and the spiritual has physical implications. Because we have been redeemed through Christ, it ought to begin changing everything. This goes beyond becoming praying people who read our Bible and worship with other Christians, although that is a start. It is a complete reorientation of our lives, our values, our prejudices, and our outward expression and activities. It means that we now treat the cashier at the grocery store with respect and dignity knowing they are stamped with the *imago dei.* We speak kind words to them, are patient when the line is long, and are encouraging when we finally pay for our groceries because we have been redeemed! We have Christ within us, therefore what we may call good works, is simply an overflow of an abundant life. I would like to propose that the way we treat the cashier says more about our life in Christ than how much we have prayed or read the Bible. I vividly remember sitting in a restaurant with a pastor of a large city church and being disgusted with the arrogance, impatience, and rudeness in which he treated the server. I was completely embarrassed. It is easy to know the right answers, have a finely sliced theology, but have zero impact or influence on our cities because we are too preoccupied with being right. Theology is indeed important but I have known too many theologically sound people who live like they are unredeemed. When we have created a false dichotomy between the physical and the spiritual, it is easy to overemphasize one and neglect the other. Metrospirituality is about walking the razor sharp line between both.

For successive generations of church planters it is absolutely essential to be metrospiritual in the core of their being. As I have reflected on this I am still not entirely sure how one gets to this place. We can parachute drop people into urban areas but that does not mean they will embrace the city and look it with spiritual eyes. It may have quite the opposite effect. For many it is a journey and a progression. In my own life it started that day I became a church planting strategist when suddenly I was responsible for seeing churches planted all over the city. I knew I had to change but did not know how. Like I previously shared, it meant for me to muster up all of my courage to begin exploring every part of the city beginning with the downtown core. The first step towards metrospirituality is to begin loving the city. That is the foundation and the basis. The reason we love the city is because God has a plan for it that goes far beyond simply us and our church. The people who live within are loved by God as we see evidenced by Jesus' sacrificial death. It is this love that acts as our foundation and it is the fuel that propels us forward. It is easy to love a city and parts of the city that are beautiful, well-maintained, and safe. When cities are undesirable, dangerous, and wild our love is truly tested.

I had a friend who lived in Baku, Azerbaijan. He had been there a number of years serving and I vividly remember him talking about praying that he would love the city. It is not the most glamorous city to love but he was praying that God would give him a supernatural love for Baku. While Tucson is nothing like Baku, I prayed continuously that God would give me a love for the city and even its built environment. Sure, the Sonoran Desert and mountains surrounding the city were breath-taking and picturesque. The actual built environment for many parts of Tucson was less than desirable and the product of rampant or haphazard sprawl. However, I loved the city and over the years it grew on me. When I would travel to other cities it was evident what Tucson was lacking but it did not matter to me because my heart was there and, to me, it was the best place on the planet. Now that we live in Vancouver, it is almost too easy to love the city with its amazing skyline and an even more impressive backdrop of snow-capped mountains and ocean.

While it may sound like an oversimplification to mention one ought to love their city, there really is no better starting place. That love moves us in a direction we may not normally take and helps us to engage this city in ways we could not previously imagine. Suddenly,  issues hit close to home in our personal lives as we feel what the city feels. Transportation has become an important topic for me and my family, whereas before it was not even on my radar. Until we moved here to Vancouver, we had lived in cities in the US where the primary way of commuting and getting around involved the use of the auto. Although that is still true here, the city has a good public transportation system which includes the Skytrain. When it came time to decide where to move, we knew it had to be in a walkable neighborhood and close to a Skytrain station. In preparation for the move, we sold one of our vehicles to better acclimate to urban life. We quickly realized the benefits of living in a mixed-use city center with ample access to the amenities we need on foot as well as rapid transit. Everything we needed was right out our door. Walking or biking everywhere became commonplace, whether it was to the grocery store, the movie theater, the coffee shop, library, and so much more. Over time we began using our car less and less until I got to the point where I was contemplating simply parking it and leaving it sit. Fortunately or unfortunately, the decision was thrust upon me when our car broke down and we ended up parking it for good. That lone circumstance began changing everything for me personally and for my family. We learned to be 100 percent dependent upon public transportation. That turned out to be an enormous blessing and has taught us much. We have been able to see so much of the city that many do not because all of a sudden we are keenly aware of how to get around the city, what to look for, connection or transfer points, and so on. On top of that, walking and biking has been good for the body, mind and soul. It offers the best glimpse of the city as well as affords ample time to observe and pray. We see many people throughout our neighborhood who live the same way and it is a way of life. As a result, when transportation issues come up in the news or in the coffee shop, my ears perk up, I listen, and I engage in conversation. Since I love the city, now city issues are my issues.

Like many church planters, all of my educational background is more in the realm of theology, biblical studies, and church planting. When I stepped into the world of seeking to understand not only my city, but cities in general, it sent me on a crash course of learning that I have been on for years now. There are numerous layers or perspectives of the city to understand with transportation being a key component. It has become important enough to weave it into the core values of the Ion Community. As I have learned the rhythms of the city of Vancouver via transit I have become more acutely aware of the issue of auto versus public transit, bikes versus the auto, the expansion of rapid transit versus freeway expansion, and many other peripheral issues. The City Program at Simon Fraser University offers free lectures on various topics that deal with urban issues ranging from design to creating sustainable communities and everything in between. One of the topics of late has been the topic of transportation. At times the university would have visiting faculty or lecturers from around the world. Through The City Program the school would offer lectures available to the public. I noticed that several of the upcoming lectures were indeed on the topic of public transportation so I signed up.

To say I was excited would be an understatement. My current reading portfolio then included topics ranging from Canadian urbanism to car-free cities to high-density cities and transportation. The academic interest combined with our personal experiences proved to be fertile soil for my own thought process. When the day of the lecture came, I rode the Skytrain to SFU's downtown campus where The City Program was housed. After I checked in I found a seat by the window that overlooked the Waterfront Station and during the course of the evening I would glance out those same windows to watch the Seabus coming and going from the downtown to the north shore. The lecture provided everything I hoped for and then some. It was fascinating being a pastor in a room of 200 others who were mostly engineers, urban planners, graduate students, and city officials. My love for the city and the issues that were of importance to Vancouver is what drove me being there. Again, this topic is so critical in my own thinking that I had made it one of the backbones of our church planting strategy as well as an overarching core value.

The whole vision and trajectory of the Ion Community is built off of Vancouver's transit system. Metrospirituality takes what the city offers and strategies are formed around it. As we make plans to start Ion Communities in the various city centers across metro Vancouver, in my mind it makes sense because everything is already in place. The city centers continue to densify as more people are opting for an urban lifestyle regardless if they live in the downtown core or 15 miles removed. These mini-downtowns are most often built at critical junctions of rapid transit usually entailing a Skytrain station. I am able to access most of the city centers on Skytrain, and in the places where it does not go, I can opt for the bus or Seabus. This expression of urbanism was one of the leading factors in choosing Vancouver over other cities in the region. This city center concept makes sense, is an attempt to decentralize and densify, and offers an urban lifestyle choice that many desire and do not need to pay downtown prices to get. Take Port Moody, for example. It is a sleepy little crescent shaped community wrapped around the eastern end of the Burrard Inlet. However, the city has a growing city center with numerous residential towers under construction and an undeniable urban feel to the place. This is the type of place where we want to plant urban-focused churches. Why? That leads into one of our core values.

Out of the 5 core values that identifies the Ion Community, one of them is related solely to transportation. I believe that if there is one value that could potentially set the Ion Community apart from many churches it is this value: Walkable. It is one thing to have it in writing and a whole different notion to actually live it out. The idea behind values is that they become drivers for the way the church is developed. It is a guiding force. So why walkable? It seems from the beginning that this is an antithesis to the way most churches develop and grow. Like I shared earlier in the book, before the advent of the auto city planners and developers planned out cities with the pedestrian in mind . . . or horse. Therefore everything was compact and mixed-use. Again, mixed-use simply means that residential and commercial coexist and are not separated. In a neighborhood it would be a common occurrence to walk to the corner market or grocery story. Since one had to walk (or ride a horse and cart) everything had to be close and accessible. Once autos entered the scene, it acted as a centrifugal force as cities rapidly expanded outward. It became (and still is) commonplace for people to drive great distances for work, shopping, and entertainment. Zoning laws changed and residential and commercial were separated to the point where we have endless rows of track homes with possibly a commercial district at the entrance of the development. Whereas it was once commonplace for people to worship with others in their neighborhood, the commuter mentality catapulted the church growth movement. Churches became regional and it is not uncommon for people to drive an hour to worship with others throughout the city. One of the challenges is the lack of ties and connections to the neighborhood. I wonder out loud whether this is one of the influencing factors as to why the church has little to no impact in culture, particularly their community. If people are driving in from all over the city, what investment is there in the area around the church? Why would someone living forty-five minutes away really care about the area where the church meets? It is drive in, worship, and then drive home. Disturbing.

Maybe this is truly a purist movement and nonsensical, but when it comes to the Ion Community, the goal is to reverse that trend by putting worshipping communities in the city centers. That it makes it accessible to those who want to simply walk or bike. My hope is this elevates the love, care, and investment in the immediate neighborhood and city center. This is what I mean by the Ion being walkable. With the focus being on a walkable church, it also ties into the idea of being an interconnected network that utilizes the existing transit system to plant churches and stay connected. This is an example of metrospirituality influencing church planting decisions by taking what the city offers. This idea never would have worked in Tucson, but in every city has the potential for unique expressions of churches to arise as they are planted in the fertile cultural soil at hand. Metrospiritual.

The tension of metrospirituality is that it is difficult to put parameters around it. I can explain at length the global urban focus of it, the implications for community transformation, and the need to hammer out a theology of the city, but it seems like it is more of an intuitive process rather than a systematic one. In some ways it is being a student of culture and more particularly that of the global city. It is amazing how the shift in mission has moved to the city over the past five years. Suddenly, many church planters are talking about the city, engaging the city, relocating into the city, and planting their lives within. It was as if one day it began clicking for many people at once. Who knows, maybe like software or hardware, this book will be irrelevant as soon as it is printed. Whereas the suburbs have been the primary landing place for church planters with the shift of thinking to the city, maybe the city is the new suburbs or will be soon. One of the primary characteristics that separates urban from suburban, though, is the density. Most current church planting training and practices are geared towards low-density suburban developments, but as our cities densify, there is a need for a new approach to church planting that is metrospiritual.

Planting churches in high-density cities or city centers is one of the cores of being metrospiritual. In these types of environments the foundational aim of loving a city is crucial. It is the same in any relationship we have whether with our spouse, children, or friends in that when love guides us we are forced live that out and not merely mouth the words. Love compels us to give sacrificially to our family and work through difficult issues. It is the same with cities, and as they continue to diversify and internationalize through immigration, enlarge through urbanization, interconnect worldwide through globalization, and densify, it will at the same time bring about peculiar issues that low-density homogeneous settings simply do not have. When there is a myriad of cultures and ethnicities living in proximity with one another in dense environments, it brings about a whole new environment to navigate in. Again, my aim is not to claim that one setting for church planting is easier than another but true multicultural and dense city centers offer unique challenges. Not only are there basic obstacles, like language, to overcome, but worldviews and religious differences make navigation not only more challenging but also enjoyable. When our boys have school friends over we always need to figure out what their background is because if they are Muslim or Sikh, for example, it means we need to ensure we have the right kind of food to eat.

As cities densify, it means that the built environment has a direct bearing on one's worldview and outlook. Geography influences people whether it is rural western Nebraska, South Beach in Florida, South Chicago, or Manhattan. There is something about dense urban environments that truly does affect the way people living there views life and other parts of the city. When I make trips out to the far flung suburbs it suddenly feels like I am in another world. Now imagine how even greater the differences ought to be in the approach to planting churches yet again. This is where we falter because of the one-size-fits all systems that we have in place. Something must change not only in regards to the way church planting is to be done in dense urban contexts, but also in the type of person the lead planter is. In many of our assessments systems we are still determining success or viability based upon still the entrepreneurial Type-A up-front charismatic personality. Many church planters already do not fit into that mold and when complex urban environments are brought into the equation, it can create tension. I suppose one of the key differences is in how church planters even see themselves: church planter or missionary? If being metrospiritual means embracing a city-centric faith that will have direct ramifications in how the city is viewed and engaged in, I believe in many ways it is more important than what an assessment says.

Assessments are great tools and are valuable to the church planting process. I am in favor of them as the tests and results do bring up valuable information for the church planter to see in how God had made them. My only struggle is the cookie-cutter church planter type that seems to have been deemed the model church planter by all others are measured. The more dense and complex the urban environment, the more varied a personality and skill set one needs to not only survive, but thrive. Without being overly simplistic there is an enormous variance in the church planter type who sees a lot of quick growth in a homogeneous suburban setting in comparison to a multicultural dense urban environment. Both are needed desperately so this is an attempt to bring to light the subtle and not so subtle differences. Some church planters are better adapted, equipped, and wired for different settings. One of the components we are missing in the assessment is in regards to the geography of church planting. Not only should we better understand who the church planters are, but even help them in determining the right environments that would be a good fit for them. The challenge, though, is when most church planting networks or denominations strongly favor the suburbs, it means assessments will be done with that setting in mind. This is where a metrospirituality kicks in …

Faith and church planting in the city is a messy yet beautiful process. Through my research and exploration of the various topics at hand there arose more questions than answers. That is good. Something like this will help move the conversation forward rather than put a tidy bow on it and say it is finished. My hope for this chapter was to begin the next step of throwing another conversational log on the fire. Here is the flow of my logic: (1) Most churches are planted in the suburbs. (2) We need more new churches in the city. (3) What is different about planting in the city compared to the suburbs? (4) We need a new way of planting churches in our urban centers that leads to community transformation and embracing the city. (5) More than simply planting churches in urban centers we need an urban theological framework to see, understand, love, and live in the city. (6) This is what it means to be metrospiritual.

## FINAL THOUGHTS

Previously, in this book I had set out some of my initial hypotheses or assumptions that I had drawn before I began the research process. Now after collecting and reviewing the data from the research and surveys, I look back on some of my suspicions and leanings. I found in many ways my hypotheses were indeed correct. There are truly more churches being started in the suburbs compared to within the city limits. That conclusion is not even debatable. However, what is debatable is the why. The bulk of a metro area's population does reside outside of the city limit and in the suburbs, so it is a logical explanation that the majority of churches are being started where the bulk of the population is. However, the why is still tricky to define even though the surveys did reveal results. Knowing that the overwhelming majority of church planters found and surveyed were Caucasian, does this fact also explain why they planted in suburban settings, which in the United States is still mostly homogenous leaning in favor of the Caucasian population? That question is for another round of exploration and research.

Throughout the research, I began to see themes as well as connection points. Some of these connectors seemed more obvious, and others again require more thorough research and data collection. What is the connection between a vibrant downtown city center with the overall health of church planting? Are church planters no different than the rest of population who are drawn to hipper and trendier cities? Did cities like Seattle led the pack for the number of church plants because of this magnetic draw? Is this also why Tucson ranked low because in comparison it does not have the broad and even global appeal of a Seattle? Another connector or theme worth exploring in the future is whether the presence of the Creative Class is any indicator of the overall health of church planting in a city since church planters would be classified in that grouping of people.

When it comes to the motivation for church planting site selection, it is something very difficult to fully explain since it deals in the realm of the spiritual. How can a researcher argue with "God's call"? It almost becomes off limits to question any further when that phrase is evoked because, how can one argue with or question God? On the other hand, it did reveal something more subterranean in that if one were to take everything at face value, then God seems to have called most church planters to culturally familiar and compatible areas mostly in Caucasian middle-class suburban contexts.

Lastly, it indeed was a challenge to gather data on gentrified neighborhoods and church planting within. In some cases it was easy to define as such and in others it was more of a challenge. Even though there were some common themes, many church planters in that setting were simply doing the best they could to reach the Creative Class with the Gospel and see community transformation take place in their neighborhoods. Maybe this fact points to the reality that when it comes to church planting, everything is contextual, even in gentrified neighborhoods. It is not about doing what another church plant is doing in a like area in a different city, but instead, going through the painstaking process of exegeting one's community and seeing more organic expressions of church arise.

Metrospiritual takes all of this in, processes it, and finds ways to love and engage the city. Welcome to the beginning of the journey.

# Bibliography

American City Business Journals, Inc. "Population Boom Seen For Downtown Denver," Denver Business Journal, http://denver.bizjournals.com/denver/stories/2005/11/14/daily18.

Berelowitz, Lance. *Dream City: Vancouver and the Global Imagination*. Vancouver: Douglas & McIntyre, 2005.

Brock, Charles. *Indigenous Church Planting*. Neosho: Church Growth International, 1994.

Campbell, Jonathan S., and Jennifer Campbell. *The Way of Jesus: A Journey of Freedom for Pilgrims and Wanderers*. San Francisco: Jossey-Bass, 2005.

City of Portland "Portland Maps," http://www.portlandmaps.com/detail.cfm?action=Census&x=7643500.123&y=682976.291.

Claiborne, Shane. *The Irresistible Revolution*. Grand Rapids: Zondervan, 2006.

Conn, Harvie. *Planting and Growing Urban Churches: From Dream to Reality*. Grand Rapids: Baker Book House, 1997.

Conn, Harvie, and Manuel Ortiz. *Urban Ministry*. Downers Grover, InterVarsity, 2010.

Dear, Michael J. *From Chicago to L.A.: Making Sense of Urban Theory*. Thousand Oaks: Sage Publications, 2002.

Downtown Phoenix Partnership. "Downtown Phoenix," http://www.downtownphoenix.com/business/toolbox/reports/search?c=1&x=25&y=4.

Downtown Seattle Association. "Downtown Seattle Association," http://www.downtownseattle.com/content/businesses/Demographics.cfm.

Driscol, Mark L., and Gerry Breshears. *Vintage Church*. Wheaton: Crossway Books, 2008.

Estep, William R. *Renaissance and Reformation*. Grand Rapids, Eerdmans, 1986.

Florida, Richard. *Cities and the Creative Class*. New York: Routledge, 2005.

———. *The Rise of the Creative Class*. New York: Basic Books, 2002.

———. *Who's Your City? How the Creative Economy Is Making Where You Live the Most Important Decision in Your Life*. New York: Basic Books, 2008.

Friedman, Thomas L. *The World Is Flat: A Brief History of the Twenty-First Century*. New York: Farrar, Straus and Giroux, 2006.

Gray, Stephen, and Trent Short. *Planting Fast-Growing Churches*. St. Charles: Church Smart Resources, 2007.

Guder, Darrell, and Lois Barrett. *Missional Church: A Vision for the Sending of the Church in North America*. Grand Rapids: Eerdmans, 1998.

Hayes, John B. *Sub-Merge*. Venture: Regal Books, 2006.

Hearn, Matt. *Common Ground in a Liquid City: Essays in Defense of an Urban Future*. Oakland: AK Press, 2010.

Hirsch, Alan. *The Forgotten Ways: Reactivating the Missional Church.* Grand Rapids: Brazos Press, 2006.

LA Inc. "L.A. Facts," Discover Los Angeles, http://www.discoverlosangeles.com/media research/la-facts#ethnic.

Lees, Loretta, et al. *Gentrification.* New York: Routledge, 2008.

Lupton, Robert D. *Renewing the City: Reflections on Community Development and Urban Renewal.* Downers Grove: InterVarsity Press, 2005.

McCallum, Dennis, and Gary DeLashmutt. "What Is the Universal Church?" Xenos, http://www.xenos.org/classes/um1-1a.html.

Merriam-Webster, Incorporated. "Gentrification," Merriam-Webster, http://www.merriam -webster.com/dictionary/gentrification.

Metro Vanvcouver. "Livable Centres," Metro Vancouver, http://www.metrovancouver.org/ planning/development/livablecentres/Pages/default.aspx.

Oldenburg, Ray. *A Great Good Place: Cafes, Coffee Shops, Bookstores, Bars, Hair Salons, and other Hangouts at the Heart of a Community.* New York: Marlow & Company, 1999.

Renn, Aaron M. "The White City," New Geography, http://www.newgeography.com/ content/001110-the-white-city.

Roberts Jr., Bob. *Glocalization: How Followers of Jesus Engage a Flat World.* Grand Rapids: Zondervan, 2007.

The City of Burnaby. "Welcome to Burnaby," The City of Burnaby, http://www.city. burnaby.bc.ca/burnaby.html.

The Marshall Foundation. "Main Gate Square," Main Gate Square, http://www.maingate square.com.

UN-Habitat. *Planning Sustainable Cities.* London: Earthscan, 2010.

Valley Metro. "Metro Light Rail," Valley Metro, http://www.valleymetro.org/metro_light_ rail.

Wikimedia Foundation, Inc. "Albuquerque, New Mexico," Wikipedia, http://en.wikipedia .org/wiki/Albuquerque,_New_Mexico.

———. "Bellevue, Washington," Wikipedia, http://en.wikipedia.org/wiki/Bellevue,_ Washington.

———. "Capital Hill," Wikipedia, http://en.wikipedia.org/wiki/Capitol_Hill,_Denver.

———. "Creative Class," Wikipedia, http://en.wikipedia.org/wiki/Creative_class.

———. "Demographics of Vancouver", Wikipedia, http://en.wikipedia.org/wiki/ Demographics_of_Vancouver.

———. "Denver," Wikipedia, http://en.wikipedia.org/wiki/Denver.

———. "Downtown Albuquerque," Wikipedia, http://en.wikipedia.org/wiki/Downtown_ Albuquerque#EDo.

———. "Forest Park," Wikipedia, http://en.wikipedia.org/wiki/Forest_Park_%28St._ Louis,_Missouri%29.

———. "Garden Cities of To-morrow," Wikipedia, http://en.wikipedia.org/wiki/Garden_ Cities_of_To-morrow.

———. "Homophily," Wikipedia, http://en.wikipedia.org/wiki/Homophily.

———. "Le Corbusier," Wikipedia, http://en.wikipedia.org/wiki/Le_Corbusier.

———. "Mesa Del Sol," Wikipedia, http://en.wikipedia.org/wiki/Mesa_del_Sol.

———. "Paolo Soleri," Wikipedia, http://en.wikipedia.org/wiki/Paolo_Soleri.

———. "Phoenix, Arizona," Wikipedia, http://en.wikipedia.org/wiki/Phoenix,_Arizona.

———. "Portland, Oregon," Wikipedia, http://en.wikipedia.org/wiki/Portland,_Oregon.

————. "Portland, Oregon Demographics," Wikipedia, http://en.wikipedia.org/wiki/ Portland,_Oregon#Demographics.

————. "Seattle," Wikipedia, http://en.wikipedia.org/wiki/Seattle.

————. "Seattle Demographics," Wikipedia, http://en.wikipedia.org/wiki/ Seattle#Demographics.

————. "South Lake Union," Wikipedia, http://www.discoverslu.com/.

————. "Tacoma, Washington," Wikipedia, http://en.wikipedia.org/wiki/Tacoma,_ Washington.

————. "Tucson, Arizona," Wikipedia, http://en.wikipedia.org/wiki/Tucson,_Arizona.

————. "Vancouver," Wikipedia, http://en.wikipedia.org/wiki/Vancouver.

Wood, Phil, and Charles Landry. *The Intercultural City: Planning for Diversity Challenge.* London: Earthscan, 2008.